Foundations of

Physical Science Investigations

Tom Hsu, Ph.D.

FIRST EDITION
Cambridge Physics Outlet
Peabody, Massachusetts 01960

The cover is an evocative montage of historical and scientific achievements that demonstrate the incredible persistence of the human intellect. Around the border, daVinci's graphics reflect an evolving tapestry of conceptual thinking as they interweave with more contemporary themes. DaVinci's fantastical mechanisms become the modern bicycle, a quintessential machine, which rolls into a graphical interpretation of wavelength division multiplexing on a fiber optic. The images follow 500 years of scientific and technological innovation. The Earth and DNA symbolize the interdependence of the built world and the natural world. The exquisite blend of form and function revealed in the elegant geometry of the chambered nautilus folds into a spiral defined by the Golden Rectangle. The interplay of organic and architectural forms represents the balance we seek between the power of technology and the fragility of our lives and our world. I hope this colorful interplay of images will inspire interest and excitement about the discovery of science.

Bruce Holloway - Senior Creative Designer

Foundations of Physical Science - Investigations
Copyright © 2002 Cambridge Physics Outlet
ISBN 1-58892-006-2
1 2 3 4 5 6 7 8 9 - QWE - 05 04 03 02 01

Cambridge Physics Outlet
26 Howley Street,
Peabody, MA 01960
(800) 932-5227
http://www. cpo.com

Printed and Bound in the United States of America

CPO SCIENCE CURRICULUM DEVELOPMENT TEAM

Tom Hsu, Ph.D – Author, President

Ph.D., Applied Plasma Physics, Massachusetts Institute of Technology

Nationally recognized innovator in science and math who has taught in middle and high school, college, and graduate programs. Personally held workshops with more than 10,000 teachers and administrators to promote teaching physics using a hands-on approach. CPO was founded by Dr. Hsu to create innovative hands-on materials for teaching math and science.

Lynda Pennell – Curriculum and Professional Development, Vice President.

B.A.English, M.Ed., Administrations, Reading Disabilities, Northeastern University; CAGS Media, University of Massachusetts, Boston

Nationally known in high school restructuring, and for integrating academic and career education. Has served as the director of an urban school, with seventeen years teaching/administrative experience, and is the author of curriculum topic materials.

Thomas Narro – Product Design, Vice President

B.S., Mechanical Engineering, Rensselaer Polytechnic Institute

Accomplished design and manufacturing engineer, experienced consultant in corporate re-engineering and industrial-environmental acoustics.

Scott Eddleman – Lead Senior Curriculum Writer

B.S., Biology, Southern Illinois University; M.Ed, Harvard University.

Taught for thirteen years in urban and rural settings; nationally known as a trainer of inquiry-based science/math project-based instruction; curriculum development consultant.

Irene Baker – Senior Curriculum Writer

B.S., Humanities, B.S. Chemistry, MIT; M.Ed. Lesley University

Experience is in scientific curriculum development, in educational research and assessment, and as a science consultant.

Laine Ives – Curriculum Writer

B.A., English, Gordon College; graduate work biology, Cornell University and Wheelock College

Experience teaching middle and high school, here and abroad, and expertise in developing middle school curriculum and hands-on activities.

Mary Beth Abel – Curriculum Writer

B.S., Marine Biology, College of Charleston; M.S., Biological Sciences, University. of Rhode Island

Taught science and math at an innovative high school; has expertise in scientific research and inquiry-based teaching methods.

Bruce Holloway – Senior Creative Designer

Pratt Institute, N.Y.; Boston Museum School of Fine Arts

Expertise in product design, advertising, and three dimensional exhibit design; winner of National Wildlife 1999 Stamp Award.

CURRICULUM CONTRIBUTORS

Thomas Altman – Teaches physics at Oswego High School, NY, and invented the Altman Method for making holograms in the classroom.

Patsy DeCoster – Curriculum specialist who taught high school science for twelve years, and has expertise in research and education technology. Conducts CPO teacher workshops.

Gary Garber – Teaches physics and math at Boston University Academy, and is a researcher at the BU Photonics Center. Past president of the Southeast section of the American Association of Physics Teachers.

Matt Lombard – Marketing manager- oversees marketing and public relations activities for CPO, expertise is in photography of equipment and curriculum materials.

Catalina Moreno – Taught for eight years at East Boston High, an inner city school, as a bilingual science/math teacher; an expert resource for American Astronomical Society.

CONSULTANTS

Julie Dalton – editor and writing consultant

Tracy Morrow – technical consultant

James Travers – illustrator and graphic designer

John Mahomet – graphic designer

Polly Crisman – illustrator and graphic designer

Dexter Beals – Beals Dynamics

Kent Dristle – Physics teacher, Oswego high school

Mike Doughty – intern, Endicott college

Jennifer Lockhart – intern, Endicott College

PRODUCT DESIGN

Jeff Casey – experimental physicist

Roger Barous – machinist

Kathryn Gavin – quality specialist

Agnes Chan – manufacturing engineer

Greg Krekorian, Shawn Greene, and Edwin Ojeda – production team

REVIEWERS

USING ICONS TO LOCATE INFORMATION

Icons are symbols that have meaning. They are small pictures that convey meaning without words. In the CPO program we use icons to point out things such as safety considerations, real-world connections, and when to find information in the reference pages, complete a writing assignment, or work in a team. The chart below lists the icons that refer to instruction and safety and the meaning for each one

	Reading: you need to read for understanding.		**Real-world connections:** you are learning how the information is used in the world today.
	Hands-on activity: you will complete a lab or other activity.		**Teamwork:** you will be working in a team to complete the activity.
	Time: Tells how much time the activity may take.		**Economics:** you are learning about how science impacts the economy.
	Research: you will need to look up facts and information.		**Formula:** you are reading information about a formula or will need to use an equation to solve a problem.
	Setup: directions for equipment setup are found here.		**Use extreme caution:** follow all instructions carefully to avoid injury to yourself or others.
	History: you are reading historical information.		**Electrical hazard:** follow all instructions carefully while using electrical components to avoid injury to yourself or others.
	Environment: you are reading information about the environment or how to protect our environment.		**Wear safety goggles:** requires you to protect your eyes from injury.
	Writing: you need to reflect and write about what you have learned.		**Wear a lab apron:** requires you to protect your clothing and skin.
	Project: you need to complete an assignment that will take longer than one day.		**Wear gloves:** requires you to protect your hands from injury due to heat or chemicals.
	Apply your knowledge: refers to activities or problems that ask you to use your skills in different ways.		**Cleanup:** includes cleaning and putting away reusable equipment and supplies, and disposing of leftover materials.

INVESTIGATION TEXT

Investigations are hands-on activities that accompany the student text. For each section of the text, you will complete a hands-on activity, answer key questions, and find results. The Investigation Manual is a soft cover book containing investigation activities that accompany each section you are reading. Sometimes you will read the student text before doing an Investigation activity, but usually you will complete the Investigation before you read the section.

The Investigations are the heart of the CPO program. We believe that you will learn and remember more if you have many opportunities to explore science through hands-on activities that use equipment to collect data and solve problems. Most of the Investigations rely on the use of CPO equipment to collect accurate data, explore possibilities and answer the key question. The equipment is easy to set up, and your teacher will help you learn how to use the equipment properly.

FEATURES OF THE INVESTIGATION

Key Question: Each Investigation starts with a key question that conveys the main focus of the learning. This question tells you what information you need to collect to answer the questions at the end of the Investigation.

Data Tables: Data tables help you organize and collect your data in a systematic manner.

Learning Objectives (Goals): At the top of each Investigation are the learning goals. These statements will explain what you will have learned and can do after completing the investigation.

Brief introduction: This information helps you understand why the exercise is important and, in most cases, how it connects to other sections you have read or will be reading.

Icons and Section title: The icon reminds you of the unit that you are studying and the section title. This section title corresponds to the reading in your Student Edition.

Numbered Steps: The Investigation sequence numbers point out the sequence of steps you will need to follow to successfully complete the Investigation. These steps highlight specific stages of the scientific method such as: following directions, completing hands-on experiments, collecting and analyzing data and presenting the results. The Applying Your Knowledge step asks you to reflect on what you have learned.

Illustrations: The illustrations support your understanding of the Investigation procedures.

Fill-in answer sheets: Your teacher will provide you with answer sheets to fill in the data tables and the written responses and may collect your information. You can also use the sheets to reinforce your reading in your student text.

INVESTIGATION PAGES

Section title reference from the student text

Section number referenced from the student text

Unit topic

Icon representing unit topic

Key question

Major learning objective for the Investigation

Explanation of Investigation content

Illustration and charts that support content

Investigation sequence numbers

Example data table*

Thought-provoking question

Detailed explanations of Investigation procedures, equipment setup, and data collection

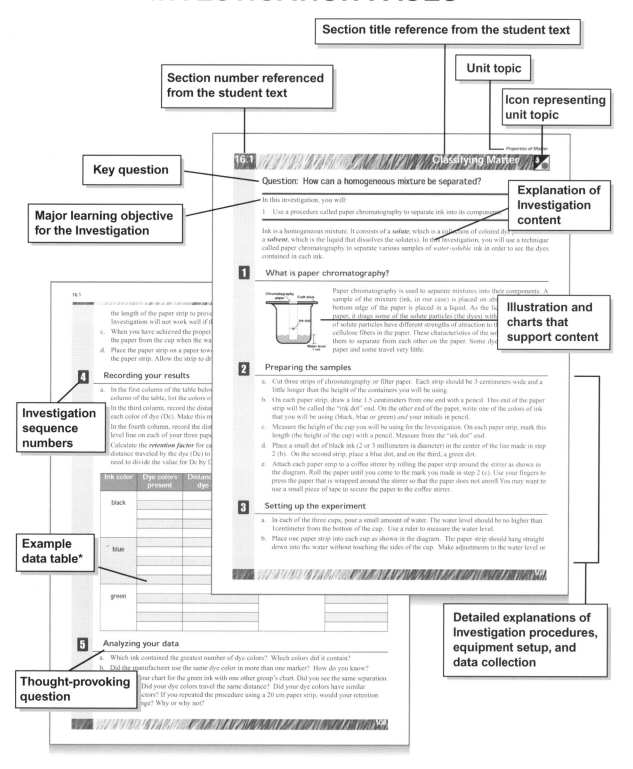

* Note: All data and answers to questions will be written on a separate fill-in answer sheet.

SAFETY

In scientific investigations, you often work with equipment and supplies. These are fun to use, especially because they help you make discoveries. However, using equipment and carrying out certain procedures in an investigation always requires safety. Safety is a very important part of doing science. The purpose of learning and discussing safety in the lab is to help you learn how to be safe at all times.

The Investigations that you will be doing as part of the CPO Integrated Physics and Chemistry curriculum are designed to reduce safety concerns in the laboratory. The physics Investigations use equipment that is stable and easy to use. The chemistry Investigations use household supplies and chemicals. Although these chemicals might be familiar to you, they still must be used safely.

You will be introduced to safety by completing a skill sheet to help you observe the safety aids and important information in your science laboratory. In addition to this skill sheet, you may be asked to check your safety understanding and complete a safety contract. Your teacher will decide what is appropriate for your class.

Throughout the Investigation Guide, safety icons and words and phrases like "caution" and "Safety Tip" are used to highlight important safety information. Read the description of each safety icon carefully and look out for them when reading your Student Edition and Investigation Guide.

⬦	**Use extreme caution:** follow all instructions carefully to avoid injury to yourself or others.
⚡	**Electrical hazard:** follow all instructions carefully while using electrical components to avoid injury to yourself or others.
👓	**Wear safety goggles:** requires you to protect your eyes from injury.
🦺	**Wear a lab apron:** requires you to protect your clothing and skin.
🧤	**Wear gloves:** requires you to protect your hands from injury due to heat or chemicals.
🪣	**Cleanup:** includes cleaning and putting away reusable equipment and supplies, and disposing of leftover materials.

Safety in the science lab is the responsibility of everyone! Help create a safe environment in your lab by following the safety guidelines from your teacher as well as the guidelines discussed in this document.

Table of Contents

UNIT 7: Changes in Matter

UNIT 8: Water and Solutions

UNIT 9: Heating and Cooling

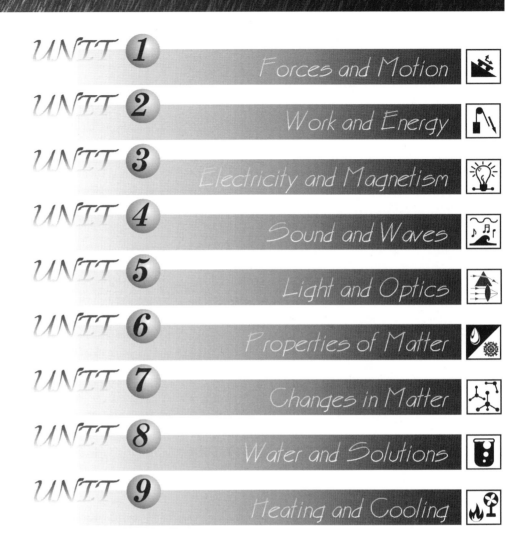

1.1 Time and Distance

Question: How do we measure and describe the world around us?

In this Investigation, you will:

1 Learn to use electronic timing equipment and photogates.
2 Use units of time in calculations and conversions.
3 Learn to read dimensioned drawings and measure quantities in metric and English units.
4 Investigate the accuracy, precision, and resolution of a scientific instrument.

1 Using the timer as a stopwatch

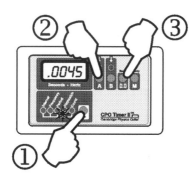

1 Set the timer to stopwatch.
2 The "A" button starts and stops the stopwatch.
3 The red "0" button resets the stopwatch to zero.

In science, it is often important to know how things change with time. The electronic timer allows us to make accurate, precise measurements of time. The timer performs many different functions. The first function to try is **stopwatch**. Use the button (1) to move the light under the word stopwatch.

A stopwatch measures a **time interval**. The stopwatch is started and stopped with the "A" button (2). The display shows time in seconds up to 60 seconds, then changes to show minutes: seconds for times longer than one minute.

The time it takes a signal to go from your brain to move a muscle is called **reaction time**. Reaction time varies from person to person and can be affected by factors like tiredness or caffeine.

From your measurements with the stopwatch, estimate the approximate reaction time of an average student.

2 Using the photogates

A photogate allows us to use a light beam to start and stop the timer. When the timer is in interval mode, it uses photogates to control the clock.

1 Select interval on the timer.
2 Connect a single photogate to the "A" input with a cord.
3 Push the "A" button and the "A" light should come on and stay on.
4 Try blocking the light beam with your finger and observe what happens to the timer. Note: The photogate has a reaction time much shorter than your finger.

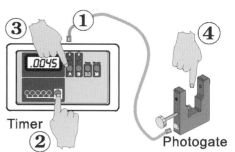

Timer

Photogate

Because it is used for so many measurements, you need to figure out how the photogate and timer work together. Try your own experiments until you can answer the following questions.

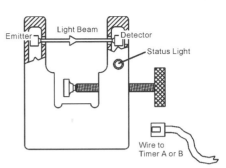

a. Exactly what do you do to start and stop the clock? Be very specific in your answer. Someone who has never see the photogate before should be able to read your answer and know what to do with the light beam to make the clock start, and what to do to make it stop.

b. If you block the light beam several times in a row does the time add or does the timer start at zero every time you break the beam? Your answer should provide observations that back up what you say. For example, "the timer does _____ because_____," where you fill in the blanks with what you think based on what you observed.

3 Using the timer with two photogate

You can connect two photogates to the timer in interval mode. The second photogate connects behind the "B" light. Notice that the "A" and "B" buttons turn the "A" and "B" lights on and off. With two photogates there are more kinds of time measurements you can make. The display shows something different for each combination of lights.

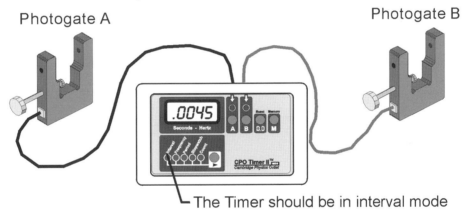

The Timer should be in interval mode

Conduct experiments to determine what stops and starts the stopwatch for each of the different combinations of lights. Write your observations as if you were trying to teach someone else how the timer works.

a. What starts and stops the timer when only the "A" light is on?

b. What starts and stops the timer when only the "B" light is on?

c. What starts and stops the timer when both "A" and "B" lights are on?

d. Does the timer still make measurements when there are no lights on?

e. What happens if you go though photogate A once and through photogate B multiple times? When answering this question, you might want to think about a race where all the runners start together but you want each runner's individual time to finish the race.

4 Reflecting on what we learned

a. *Resolution* means the smallest interval which can be measured. Try using one photogate to determine the resolution of the timer. Give your answer in seconds and tell how your observations support your answer.

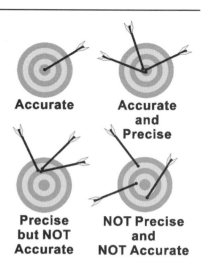

Accurate

Accurate and Precise

b. The words *accuracy* and *precision* have special meanings in science that are a little different from how people use these words every day. The word accuracy refers to how close a measurement is to the true value. The word precision describes how close together repeated measurements are. When measurements are precise they are close to the same value. It is possible to be precise but not accurate. Which is likely to be more precise: time measurements made with a stopwatch or measurements made with photogates?

Precise but NOT Accurate

NOT Precise and NOT Accurate

5 Dimensions and diagrams

Think about how often you have to describe how big something is or where something is. People say a picture is worth a thousand words. Because pictures are so much better at describing location or size, people have developed a language of pictures to communicate length or position. Learning to read diagrams is important in science. It is also important in everyday life because diagrams explain how to put together almost every product you buy that requires assembly.

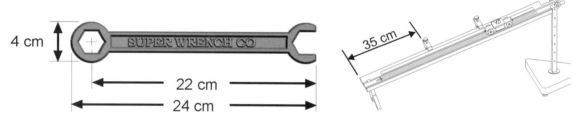

4 cm   SUPER WRENCH CO   35 cm

22 cm

24 cm

Drawings with little lines and arrows indicate distance or size. The lines, arrows, and numbers are called *dimensions*, and they tell you how big and where things are. In the example, the length of the wrench is 24 centimeters. The center of the hole in the wrench is 22 centimeters from one end. The round end has a diameter of 4 centimeters. The photogate is placed 35 centimeters from the end of the ramp.

a. Measure the dimensions of the car and the photogate as shown on the diagram. Write the dimensions in the appropriate boxes.

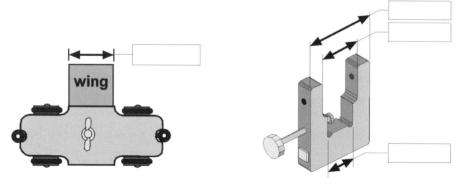

wing

6   ## Measuring metric lengths

Use the metric ruler to make measurements of each of the following dimensions. Write the measurement in centimeters in the appropriate box. You should be accurate to the nearest millimeter (0.1 centimeters).

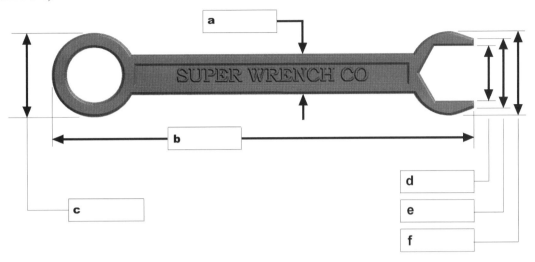

7   ## Measuring English lengths

Use the English ruler to make measurements of each of the following dimensions. Write the measurement in inches in the appropriate box. You should be accurate to the nearest 1/16th inch.

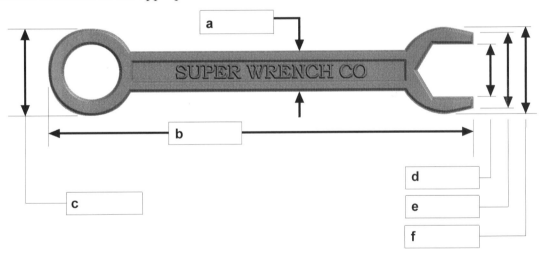

1.2 Investigations and Experiments

Question: How do we ask questions and get answers from nature?

In this Investigation, you will:

1   Use the electronic timer and photogates with a car and ramp.
2   Identify the variables that influence how fast a car travels down a ramp.
3   Learn how to design experiments that provide good scientific results.

We do experiments to collect evidence that allows us to unravel nature's puzzles. You can think of an experiment as asking a question about the universe: "What would happen if I did this?" If your experiment is well planned, the results of the experiment provide the answer you are looking for. If your experiment is not planned correctly, you will still get results but you may not know what they mean. In this Investigation, you will experiment with speed and the angle of a ramp. Only by paying careful attention to the variables can you make sense of your results.

1 Setting up the experiment

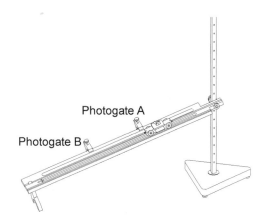

Photogate A

Photogate B

The faster you go, the shorter the time it takes. With two photogates you can measure time very accurately.

Set up the ramp and car as instructed by your teacher. Each group in the class will have a different ramp angle. The angle is determined by which hole in the stand you use to attach the ramp.

Put two photogates on the ramp so that you can measure time for the car. Plug the photogate closest to the top of the ramp into input A of the timer and the other photogate into input B.

a.   Look around the class and note which hole each group is using for its ramp. With your group, make a prediction as to which group will have the fastest car, and therefore the shortest time from A to B. This prediction is your group's hypothesis. Write down this hypothesis so you can compare it to your results.

b.   Roll the car down the ramp and record the time it takes to go from photogate A to photogate B. Be sure you look at the timer reading with the A and B lights on.

c.   Compare your results with other groups'. Did the times that everyone measured agree with your hypothesis about how the angle of the ramp would affect the speed? Why or why not?

d.   Is there a better way to test whether increasing the ramp angle makes the car go faster? Explain how you would redo this experiment so the results make sense.

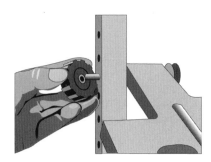

2   Variables in an experiment

Variables are the factors that affect experimental results. In part 1, each group did the experiment with too many differences, not just the angle of the ramp. That made it hard to compare results. In an experiment, you have to keep everything the same, and only change one variable at a time. If you only change one thing at a time, when you get a result you know it was caused by the variable you changed.

a. What variables will affect how fast the car moves down the ramp? List all the variables discussed by your group.

3   Doing a controlled experiment

In this part of the Investigation, you will repeat the time measurements of the car, but as you will see, each group will attach the photogates in the same way. This will allow groups to more accurately compare results.

The two distances you need to control

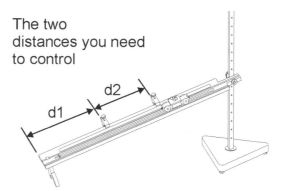

1   Use a ruler and measure and record any variables you think should be controlled to make the experiment a comparison of how cars behave on ramps of different angles.

2   Develop a good technique for rolling the car down the ramp so you get three times that are within 0.0005 seconds of each other.

3   Using your new technique and setup, record the time it takes the car to travel from photogate A to photogate B.

Once you have your new results, compare them with the rest of the class's.

a. Did your times agree with your hypothesis about how they would change with the angle of the ramp?

b. In one or two sentences describe why this experiment was better or worse than your first experiment. Your answer should talk about cause and effect relationships and variables.

The values for the variables in the experiment

Variable	Chosen value

4   Applying what you learned

a. It is often easy to confuse cause and effect. When we see something happen, we think up a reason for why it happened, but we don't always get the right reason. If you drop a piece of paper and a steel weight at the same time, which one hits the ground first? If the paper is flat, the steel always hits first. Why does the steel hit first? Is it because heavier objects fall faster, or is there another reason? In your answer give at least one other reason why a steel weight might fall faster than a flat sheet of paper.

b. Plan and perform another experiment to test the effect of one of the other variables on the speed of the car. Create a data table and a procedure for controlling the variables you don't want to change.

1.3 **Speed**

Question: What is speed and how is it measured?

In this Investigation, you will:

1   Learn how to calculate the speed of a car traveling down a ramp.
2   Compare speeds in different units.

In this Investigation, you will precisely measure how fast a car moves down a ramp and learn how to calculate its speed in different units.

1 How is speed measured?

Suppose you run a race. How do you describe your run to a friend? Saying that you ran for 20 minutes would not be enough for your friend to know how fast you went. What your friend needs in order to know how fast you went is your **speed**.

You need two elements in order to describe your speed:

*   The **distance** you traveled.

*   The **time** it took you.

Examples of speed	Calculating speed
A sprinter running 100 meters in 10 seconds (speed is 10 m/sec). A person driving a car 50 miles in 1 hour (speed is 50 mi/hr). A fish swimming 10 feet in 15 seconds (speed is 0.67 ft/sec).	a. Use the distances and time values in the examples to calculate speed. If your answers are correct, then you understand how to calculate speed. b. Your hair grows 0.4 millimeters per day. What is the speed of hair growth per week? Per hour?

2 Calculating the speed of the car on the ramp

1   Set up the car and ramp with two photogates that are one foot apart. Measure the distance from the lower edge of one photogate to the lower edge of the next photogate.

2   Measure the distance between photogates in centimeters and record the value in the table below.

3   Measure the distance between photogates in inches and record it also.

4   Make sure that the timer's A and B lights are both on. Roll the car down the ramp and measure the time it takes the car to go from photogate A to photogate B. Record the value in the table under Time from A to B *in all three rows*, since they are all the same time.

Measure distance from lower edge to lower edge.

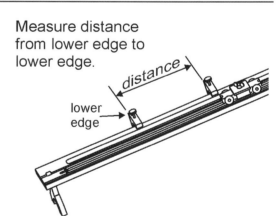

Speed, Distance, and Time Data

Distance from A to B	Time from A to B (sec)	Speed
(feet)		(feet/sec)
(cm)		(cm/sec)
(inches)		(in/sec)

Calculate the speed of your car in ft/sec, cm/sec, and in/sec and write the results in the table.

a.   Which is the fastest speed of the three, or are they all the same speed?

b.   Is it possible that a speed of 254 and a speed of 100 could be the same speed? Explain why you think so and why giving a speed as 254 would not be a very good answer.

3   ## Experiments with downhill motion

Design and conduct three experiments using the car and ramp. Each experiment should look at one variable that you think will have an effect on the speed of the car. In your lab notebook, describe what you will change and how you will determine the speed of the car in each of your three experiments.

Each experiment you do should be described in the following way in your lab notebook. You may use the Sample Lab Record and Data Table below as a guide.

a.   Hypothesis: A sentence describing what you think your experiment should demonstrate.

b.   Procedure: A few sentences describing how you did your experiment.

c.   Measurements: Data that you took including your calculations of speed.

d.   Conclusions: Answer the following questions in your conclusions: What was the outcome of the experiment? Did the outcome support your hypothesis or suggest a different hypothesis?

Be prepared to give a brief presentation to the rest of the class.

Sample Lab Record:

Hypothesis:

Variable to be tested:

Procedure:

Conclusions:

Sample Data Table:

Trial	Experimental Variable	Distance	Time	Speed
1				
2				
3				

2.1 Using a Scientific Model to Predict Speed

Question: Can you predict the speed of the car at any point on the ramp?

In this Investigation, you will:

1 Determine the speed of the car at different points as it rolls down the ramp.
2 Make a speed vs. position graph with your collected data.
3 Predict speed at any point on the ramp by using your graph.

What happens to the speed of the car as it rolls down the ramp? You can answer this question by measuring its speed at different points. By making a graph of the car's speed according to its position, you can see how speed changes. This graph can be used to predict how fast the car will be moving anywhere on the ramp. Record your observations and data from the Investigation in your notebook.

1 Finding the speed of the car at different points along the ramp?

Using two photogates far apart gives you a measure of the average speed of the car between the photogates. The car could be going faster at the lower photogate and slower at the upper one. To get a true picture of how the speed of the car changes, you will need to measure the speed with one photogate.

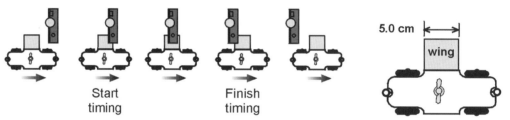

Remember, with one photogate the timers measure the time that the beam is broken. As the car passes through the photogate, the light beam is broken for the width of the wing. The speed of the car is the width of the wing (distance traveled) divided by the time it takes to pass through the light beam (time taken). The advantage to this technique is that it is easy to move a single photogate up and down the ramp to make measurements of the speed at many places.

$$\text{speed} = \frac{\text{width of wing}}{\text{time through photogate}}$$

1 Select between 5 and 10 locations along the ramp to measure the speed of the car. The places should be at regular intervals such as every 10 centimeters.
2 At each location record the position of the photogate and the time through the light beam. The distance traveled will be the same for every position since it is the width of the wing.
3 Calculate the speed of the car using the car wing length (5 cm) and the time measurement. Record this value in the table.

Speed, Position, and Time Data

Position of photogate A (cm) from top of ramp	Time from photogate A (sec)	Distance traveled by car (cm) Wing width (5 cm)	Speed of the car (cm/sec)

2 | graph | **Graphing and analyzing your results**

a. Do you notice a trend in your measurements? How does the speed of the car change as it moves down the ramp?

b. Graph the speed of the car vs. position. Place speed of the car on the *y*-axis and position of photogate A on the *x*-axis. Add labels to each axis and title the graph.

c. What does the graph show about the speed of the car?

3 **Using your graph to predict the speed of the car**

a. Choose a spot on the ramp where you did not measure the speed of the car.

b. Use your graph to find the predicted speed of the car at that distance. Record your predicted speed.

c. Place the photogate at the distance you selected in step A and record the time it takes for the car to pass through the photogate.

d. Use the wing length (5 cm) and the time to calculate the speed. Record the actual speed.

e. How does the predicted speed compare with the actual measured speed? What does this tell you about your experiment and measurements?

4 **Calculating percent error**

a. Find the difference between the predicted speed and the actual, calculated speed.

   Predicted speed − Actual speed = Difference

b. Take this difference and divide it by the predicted speed, then multiply by 100.

   (Difference ÷ Predicted speed) × 100 = Percent error

c. Use the percent error to calculate percent correct.

   100 − Percent error = Percent correct

2.2 Position and Time

Question: How do you model the motion of the car?

In this Investigation, you will:

1 Model the motion of the car with a distance vs. time graph.

2 Measure the slope of your distance vs. time graph at 3 different points.

3 Determine the relationship between slope and speed of the car.

In this Investigation, you will rely on information you have learned from working with the car and ramp to help you model the motion of the car with a distance vs. time graph. By measuring how long it takes the car to reach different points on the ramp, you be able to create a picture of the car's trip down the ramp.

1 Setting up the experiment

1 Put photogate A near the top of the ramp, but not so high that the car breaks the light beam before you let it go. Keep photogate A in this spot for the whole experiment. If you move the gate, your experiments won't be as accurate as they could be.

2 Put photogate B lower than photogate A, so the car rolls through photogate A and then through photogate B.

3 Move photogate B to between 5 and 8 different places along the ramp and record the position and times for each place.

2 Understanding and using Table I

As you measure the time it takes the car to travel to different positions, you will record your data in Table 1 on the next page. The table headings are explained below.

✏ Keep good records; you will use the data you collect in the next two Investigations.

a. **Distance from A to B:** Measure and record the distance from photogate A to photogate B.

b. **Time from A to B:** This is the time it takes the car to travel from A to B. Record the time from the timer with both A and B lights on.

c. **Time at A:** Record the time from the timer with the A light on.

d. **Time at B:** Record the time from the timer with the B light on.

e. **Speed at A:** This is the speed of the car when it passed through photogate A. Calculate this by dividing the width of the wing (5 centimeters) by the time through photogate A.

f. **Speed at B:** This is the speed of the car when it passed through photogate B. Calculate this by dividing the width of the wing (5 centimeters) by the time through photogate B.

3   Collecting and recording your data

- Release the car the same way each time to get good results.

- Move photogate B in equal increments (i.e., every 5 or 10 centimeters) so that your data will be easier to graph.

- Remember that both light beams on the timer should be clear before you press reset.

- Be careful at the bottom of the ramp. If the car bounces up when it hits the end, it may bounce back through the light beam. You will not get accurate results because your time will be wrong.

Position on ramp	Distance from A to B	Time from A to B (t_{AB})	Time at A (t_A)	Time at B (t_B)	Speed at A	Speed at B
	(cm)	(sec)	(sec)	(sec)	(cm/sec)	(cm/sec)
1						
2						
3						
4						
5						
6						
7						
8						

4   Graphing and analyzing your data

a. Make a distance vs. time graph using your data. Plot the time from A to B on the *x*-axis and the distance from A to B on the *y*-axis. At this point, do not connect the data points on the graph. Be sure to label the axes and title the graph.

b. Is the graph a straight line or a curve?

c. Does the graph get steeper as the car rolls farther, or does the graph keep the same slope the whole way? What does your answer tell you about the speed of the car at different times along its roll down the ramp?

d. Pick two points near the bottom of the graph and two more near the top of the graph. Draw two triangles and figure the speed from the slope of the graph. Is the value you get consistent with other speed measurements you have made with the car and ramp?

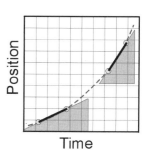

2.3 Acceleration

Question: How is the speed of the car changing?

In this Investigation, you will:

1 Determine the rate of acceleration of the car on the ramp through a calculation.
2 Determine the rate of acceleration of the car on the ramp using a graph.

For this Investigation, you will examine the data you collected from Investigation 2.2 with the car and ramp. Using your data, you will determine the rate of acceleration of the car in two ways: through calculation using an equation, and with a graph by taking the slope of the line.

Before beginning the Investigation, define the term "acceleration" in your own words. It may help you to think about flying in an airplane. When a plane is accelerating, you feel its motion. For example, you feel the motion of the plane when it is taking off, but not much when you are flying at altitude.

1 Measuring acceleration

Acceleration is the rate at which the speed changes. For the car on the ramp, the change in speed is the difference between the speed at photogate B and the speed at A. The change in time is the time from A to B. You can calculate acceleration by dividing the change in speed by the change in time.

$$acceleration = \frac{speed\ at\ B - speed\ at\ A}{time\ from\ A\ to\ B}$$

1 Put photogate A about 30 centimeters from the top of the ramp and photogate B another 20-30 centimeters farther down. Leave both photogates in the same position for the rest of the experiment.

2 Set the ramp at the same angle as you used for the last Investigation so you can compare the data.

3 With the timer in interval mode, roll the car down the ramp and record the three times (t_A, t_B, and t_{AB}) in Table 1.

4 Calculate the speeds at points A and B, and the acceleration of the car from the acceleration formula above.

5 Move the photogates to a new position and repeat the procedure to measure the acceleration.

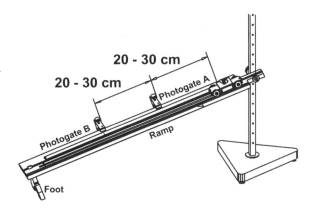

	Trial I	Trial 2
Time A		
Time B		
Time A to B		
Speed at A		
Speed at B		
Acceleration		

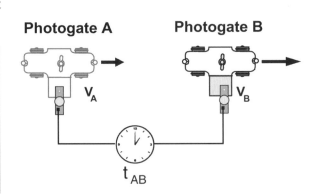

2 Graphing speed vs. time

a. Make a speed vs. time graph. Plot the speed at photogate B on the *y*-axis. Plot the time from A to B on the *x*-axis.

b. Is your graph a straight line or a curve?

c. The place on the speed vs. time graph where the line crosses the *y*-axis is called the *y*-intercept. On the speed vs. time graph for the car and ramp, the *y*-intercept represents something about the car. What is the *y*-intercept of your speed vs. time graph? (Hint: The *y*-axis is speed.)

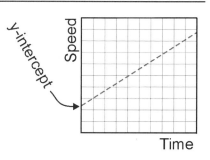

d. Does the car accelerate as it rolls down the ramp? Justify your answer. Remember that acceleration is defined as a change in speed over time.

3   Calculating acceleration from the slope of the line

In a speed vs. time graph, you are showing the change in speed over time. The slope of the speed vs. time graph is equal to the *acceleration* of the car.

a. Using your speed vs. time graph, calculate the acceleration of the car from the slope of the line. Refer to page 35 of the Student Edition for an example of the calculation. Show all of your work.

b. Is the acceleration of the car changing as it moves down the ramp? Explain your answer using what you know about the slope of a straight line.

Acceleration from the slope of the speed versus time graph

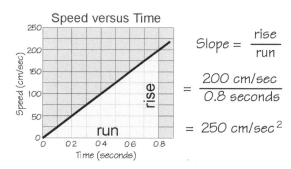

$$\text{Slope} = \frac{\text{rise}}{\text{run}}$$

$$= \frac{200 \text{ cm/sec}}{0.8 \text{ seconds}}$$

$$= 250 \text{ cm/sec}^2$$

4   Reflecting on what we learned

a. How does the acceleration you measured compare with the acceleration you calculated from the graph of speed vs. time? If there are differences, try to think where they might have come from.

b. Give the car a gentle push up the ramp from the bottom. The car will go up, slow down, and come down again. Is there a place in the motion where the speed of the car is zero? Is there a place where the acceleration is zero?

c. Can you think up two configurations of ramps and cars that show the following properties:
   (1) Higher speed but lower acceleration.
   (2) Lower speed but higher acceleration.
   You should discuss this with your group or the class. You can also test out your ideas, or draw them in sketches. (Hint: The car may not always be in the same place!)

3.1 Force, Mass, and Acceleration

Question: What is the relationship between force, mass, and acceleration?

In this Investigation, you will:

1   Measure the force on a car as it starts to roll down the ramp.
2   Compare the force on the car as the angle of the ramp is changed.
3   Calculate the acceleration of the car as the angle of the ramp is changed.
4   Explore the relationship between force and acceleration.
5   Derive Newton's second law of motion.

It takes the application of force to get an object moving. As early as Aristotle's time, in the third century BC, philosophers were seeking the relationship between force and motion. It was not until 2000 years later (1686) when Newton published the **_Principia_** that this riddle was solved by his second law of motion. In this Investigation, you follow in Newton's footsteps and figure out the relationship between force and mass and acceleration.

1   Thinking about force

To examine the relationship between force and mass and acceleration, you will use the car and ramp because it is easy to measure acceleration. In this Investigation, the variable that you will change is the force on the car. You want to find out how changing the force affects the motion. Before you begin the experiment, answer the following questions.

a.   What are the ways you can change the amount of force acting to pull the car down the ramp? Keep in mind that force is something which has the ability to change motion.

b.   How will you vary the force on the car for this experiment?

Record your ideas in your lab notebook.

2   Measuring the force on the car

1   Set up the car and ramp. Add one weight to the car.
2   Tie a short piece of string to the eye on the car. Make a loop in the other end of the string to attach to the force scale. Using a short piece of string will help you measure force accurately.

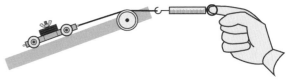

3   Read the scale while letting the car roll slowly down the ramp a short way. The scale measures force in units of newtons. Measuring while rolling down partly corrects for the effects of friction.

◆ **Safety Tip: Keep your fingers away from the ramp when the car is rolling. It is especially important to keep your hands away from the bottom of the ramp until the car stops.**

3   ## Conducting the experiment

1   Put photogate A about 30 centimeters from the top of the ramp and photogate B another 20-30 centimeters farther down. Leave both photogates in the same position for the rest of the experiment.

2   Measure the amount of force on the car using the method described in step 1. Record your results in newtons in Table 1 (see below).

3   With the timer in interval mode, roll the car down the ramp and record the three times (t_A, t_B, and t_{AB}) in Table 1.

4   Using a balance, find the mass of your car.

5   Calculate the speeds at photogates A and B, and the acceleration of the car (see acceleration formula below). Write your results in Table 1.

6   Change the angle of the ramp and repeat steps 2 - 4.

7   You may also change the mass by adding or subtracting weights.

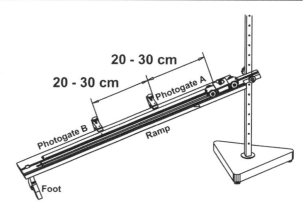

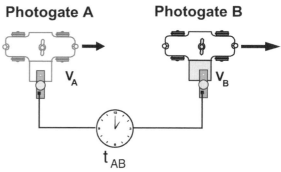

$$acceleration = \frac{speed\ at\ B - speed\ at\ A}{time\ from\ A\ to\ B}$$

$\frac{a}{b}$ **Calculating acceleration**: The acceleration is calculated from the change in speed divided by the change in time. V_B represents the speed at photogate B and V_A represents the speed at photogate A.

Table 1: Force and acceleration at different ramp angles

Mass	Force	Time A	Time B	Time A to B	Speed A	Speed B	Accel.
(kg)	(N)	(sec)	(sec)	(sec)	(m/sec)	(m/sec)	(m/sec^2)

4   ## Analyzing the data

    a. List three observations you can make about the data from looking at Table 1.

    b. The relation between force and motion is simple but not obvious. Can you see it from the data table? Write a sentence to describe your ideas about the relationship between force and motion.

5   ## Combining force and mass

In order to identify the relationship between force, mass, and acceleration, you must first make a line graph of the data. Since a graph can only show two numbers, we will be mathematically grouping the force and mass values. Different combinations of force and mass will be graphed on the x-axis and acceleration will be graphed on the y-axis.

    a. In your lab notebook, write the combination of force and mass that has been assigned to your group below. The different combinations of force and mass that we will test are:
        (1) force ÷ mass
        (2) mass ÷ force
        (3) force + mass
        (4) force × mass

    b. Transfer your force and acceleration data from Table 1 to Table 2 below. Add the mass data to this table. Using this data, make the calculations for your group's force and mass combination. Add these calculations to Table 2.

    c. We use graphs to find relationships. One or more of the graphs should show a pattern we can understand. If we find a pattern in the graph then we know the relationship between the variables from that graph is the one we want.

    d. Use the data in Table 2 to make a graph that shows the relationship between force, mass, and acceleration. Plot your group's combination of force and mass on the x-axis. Plot acceleration on the y-axis. Be sure to give a title to your graph and label the axes.

Table 2: Force, Mass, and Acceleration Data

a (acceleration) m/sec²	F (force) N	m (mass of the car) kg	force and mass calculation:

6   **Analyzing all of the graphs**

Direct relationship
Straight line

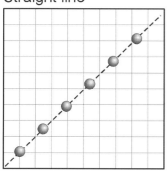

Inverse relationship
Straight line

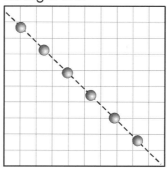

No relationship

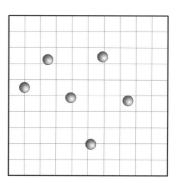

Direct relationship
Curve

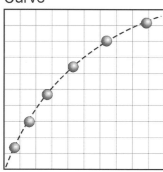

Inverse relationship
Curve

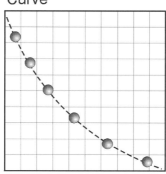

Examine all four graphs generated by your class. For each, indicate a pattern, if any, that you observe for the questions below:

a. **force ÷ mass:** Is there a pattern? If so, what is it?

b. **mass ÷ force:** Is there a pattern? If so, what is it?

c. **force + mass:** Is there a pattern? If so, what is it?

d. **force × mass:** Is there a pattern? If so, what is it?

7   **Newton's second law**

Based on this experiment, what is the correct mathematical relationship between the variables force (F), mass (m), and acceleration (a)? Write the equation and explain how you arrived at your answer.

3.2   Weight, Gravity, and Friction

Question: How does increasing the mass of the car affect its acceleration?

In this Investigation, you will:

1   Explore how added weight affects a car's acceleration.

2   Discuss and learn whether or not heavier objects fall faster than lighter objects.

3   Investigate friction and how friction affects motion.

So far in this unit, you have learned that the car accelerates as it moves down the ramp. That is, its speed increases over time. In Investigation 3.1, you explored what happened to the acceleration of a car when more force was applied to it.

The force that you used in Investigation 3.1 was gravity. Gravity pulls all objects toward the center of Earth with a force we call weight. The more mass an object has, the greater its weight. If you increase the weight of the car, how will acceleration be affected? Do heavier objects fall faster than lighter ones?

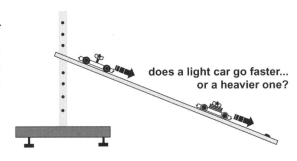

does a light car go faster...
or a heavier one?

1   **Do you think adding weights to the car will change its speed?**

a.   You can add up to three weights to the car for this experiment. Weights are attached to the top of the car using the wing nut.

b.   Roll a car down the ramp with different amounts of weight and watch it, without using photogates. Does the change in mass seem to make a difference in the speed?

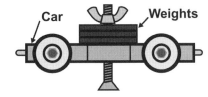

Car   Weights

Safety tip: Keep your fingers away from the ramp when the car is rolling. Especially, keep your hands away from the bottom of the ramp until the car stops.

2   **Testing your hypothesis**

It is difficult to know for sure that the car is going faster (or not) without making measurements. Set up the car and ramp with two photogates. The photogates should be about 20 centimeters apart. Set the angle at the seventh hole from the bottom of the stand.

You will want to measure the mass of the car with no weights, and with one, two, and three weights. On the data table, record the masses and the speeds at which the car rolled between the two photogates.

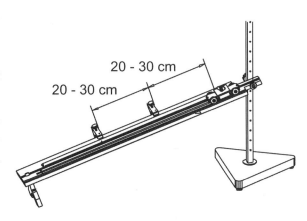

20 - 30 cm

20 - 30 cm

| Mass and Speed Data | | | |
Mass (g)	Distance from A to B (cm)	Time from A to B (sec)	Speed (cm/sec)

3 Graphing and analyzing the data

a.   Make a graph of speed vs. mass using your data.

b.   Which is the dependent variable? On which axis does it go?

c.   Which is the independent variable? On which axis does it go?

d.   From your graph, what can you say about the effect of increasing mass on the speed of the car? Did the speed change by a lot or by a little? Did the mass change by a lot or a little?

4 Friction

Try the following experiment. Take a steel weight and a flat sheet of paper. Drop them both and the steel weight will hit the ground before the paper every time. Next, crumple the sheet of paper and do the experiment over. They should hit the ground about the same time.

a.   The crumpled paper has the same weight as the flat sheet of paper. What is the explanation for why the crumpled sheet fell fast and the flat sheet fell slowly?

b.   The car has friction, even though the wheels have ball bearings. Can you think of a way to increase the friction in the car? See if you can create enough friction so the car does not accelerate, but keeps the same speed from one photogate to the next.

5 Thinking about the results

Suppose you have a jar of 1,000 marbles. If you lose one marble, it is hard to notice because 1 out of 1,000 is a small change. If you only had 5 marbles in the jar, you would immediately notice if one were missing because 1 out of 5 is a much larger change.

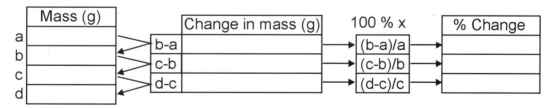

a.   We often express change in percent. One out of 5 is a change of 20 percent ($1/5 \times 100\%$). The percent change is the change divided by what you started with, times 100 percent. Calculate the percent change for the weight experiment.

b.   Does the percent change have anything to do with how much the speed changed as you added the second and third weights?

3.3 Equilibrium, Action, and Reaction

Question: What is Newton's third law of motion?

In this Investigation, you will:

1   Learn how Newton's third law of motion applies to the physics of how objects work.
2   Use your understanding of Newton's third law to find the forces in a system.

In this Investigation you will learn that Newton's third law of motion explains the physics of common objects and activities. All forces come in pairs and that means whenever we push something, there is a reaction pushing back on us.

1 Setting up a system with action and reaction

You will need a car and ramp setup, some string, and some weight as shown in the diagram. Add weight and (or) change the angle of the ramp until you get the car balanced so it moves neither up nor down the ramp.

String

Weight

a.   The car wants to roll down, and the weight also wants to fall down. Draw a sketch showing the forces that act on the car and the forces that act on the weight.

b.   Since nothing is moving, the acceleration is zero. What does this tell you about the forces acting on the car and on the weight?

c.   Suppose you added a little more hanging weight. What would happen to the system? In your answer you should discuss balanced and unbalanced forces.

d.   Suppose you took away a little from the hanging weight. What would happen to the system? In your answer you should discuss balanced and unbalanced forces.

e.   On your force sketch, label the action and reaction forces acting on the car and on the weight.

2 Equilibrium at constant speed

Set up the ramp on the lowest hole in the stand. Using the foot, you can make the ramp completely level. When the ramp is level, gravity does not act to pull the car one way or the other. Attach two photogates to the level ramp about 20 centimeters apart.

Give the car a push and use the photogates to tell whether it is speeding up or slowing down. Raise the foot end of the ramp until you can roll the car through both photogates and get the same time through each one. If the time to go through each is the same, then the speed is also the same.

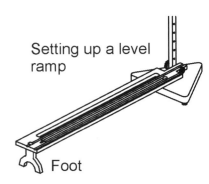

Setting up a level ramp

Foot

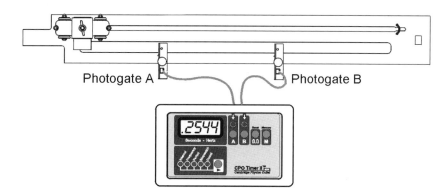

To check the time, you want to look at the time through A and the time through B, with only one light on at a time.

a. Earlier you learned that there is always friction when things are moving. If the speed is the same at A and B, then the acceleration must be zero. If the acceleration is zero, the net force must also be zero. Explain how your process of shimming up the ramp created equilibrium of forces.

b. If friction acting on the car is the action force, what is the reaction force and what object does it act on? (Hint: The object is not moving.)

3   Using Newton's third law to explain the physics of common objects and activities

a. List five objects you use on a day-to-day basis. List five activities you do on a weekly basis.

b. Next to each item on your lists, write down how the activities you do and the objects you use illustrate Newton's third law of motion. Identify an action force and a reaction force for each object and situation.

Examples of the third law

Daily things	How the third law applies	Weekly activities	How the third law applies

4   What did you learn?

a. Write Newton's third law in your own words.

b. Imagine if Newton's third law of motion was just like a law made by your government. Also, imagine there is going to be a vote tomorrow on whether to keep Newton's third law or change the universe so we did not always have an equal and opposite reaction to every action force. Think up one strange scenario that might happen if the universe changed so that the third law were not true. You may wish to do this as a project jointly with your group.

4.1 **Forces in Machines**

Question: How do simple machines work?

In this Investigation, you will:

1 Build a simple machine using ropes and pulleys.
2 Measure the input and output forces of simple machines.

Would you believe that a small child could lift an elephant with only muscle power? It's true! You could do it by building a simple machine called a block and tackle, using some ropes and pulleys. In this Investigation, you will learn how to build machines that allow you to lift large weights with small forces. You will also learn how to measure the input and output forces of these machines.

1 Identifying input and output forces

Watch a demonstration of a block and tackle machine made with ropes and pulleys.

a. What is the definition of a simple machine?

b. With your class, brainstorm additional examples of simple machines. For each machine you come up with, identify the input and output force.

2 Setting up the ropes and pulleys

1 Attach four weights to the bottom block. Use a force scale to obtain the weight of the bottom block after you attach the weights and record the weight. Weight of bottom block: _____ N

2 The output force of this simple machine will be used to lift the bottom block. Attach the top block near the top of the physics stand. The yellow string can be clipped to either the top block or the bottom block. Start with the yellow string clipped to the bottom block.

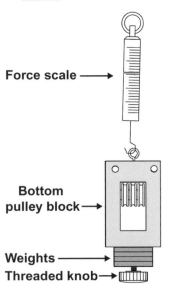

Force scale ⟶

Bottom pulley block ⟶

Weights ⟶
Threaded knob ⟶

Why all the strings?

- The yellow string will be used to move the bottom pulley block with the weights up and down. You will pull on one end of the yellow string. There is a clip at the other end of the yellow string for attaching to the pulley blocks.

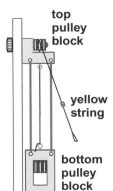

top pulley block

yellow string

bottom pulley block

- The yellow string may have several strands that directly support the bottom pulley block. These are called the supporting strands.

- The pink string is the safety string. It holds up the bottom block while you rearrange the yellow string.

⬥ **Safety Tip: Don't pull sideways or you can tip the stand over!**

3   ## Investigating the block and tackle

1   Clip the end of the yellow string to the bottom pulley block. Pass the string over the middle pulley of the top block. Use the marker stop (cord stop) to hook the force scale to the string.

2   Measure the force it takes to slowly lift the bottom pulley block.

3   This arrangement has one strand supporting the bottom pulley block. Record the force in the table below in the row corresponding to one strand.

4   Take the yellow string off and clip the end to the top block next. Pass the string around the middle pulley in the bottom block and back over the middle pulley in the top block.

5   Move the marker and measure the force it takes to slowly lift the bottom pulley block. Record this force in the row for two supporting strands.

6   Rearrange the yellow strings so that you get three, four, five, and six supporting strands. Measure and record the force it takes to lift the bottom pulley block for each new setup.

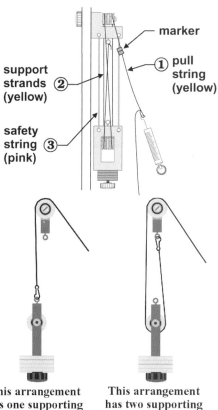

This arrangement has one supporting strand

This arrangement has two supporting strands

Number of support strands	Force to lift bottom pulley block (N)
1	
2	
3	
4	
5	
6	

a.   As you add more supporting strands, what happens to the force needed to lift the bottom block?

b.   How does the amount of input force required to lift the bottom block change with the string arrangement? Can you identify a mathematical rule?

4   ## What did you learn?

a.   How are all simple machines alike? How is a lever different from a block and tackle machine? (Think about input and output force.)

b.   What is the relationship between the number of strings on the block and tackle and the amount of input force required to lift the bottom block?

4.2

The Lever

Question: How does a lever work?

In this Investigation, you will:

1   Use a lever and describe its parts.
2   Analyze how a lever manipulates force.
3   Explore the concept of equilibrium in simple machines.

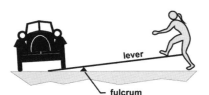

How can you lift up a car – or even an elephant – all by yourself? One way is with a lever. The lever is an example of a simple machine.

1 ## Setting up the lever

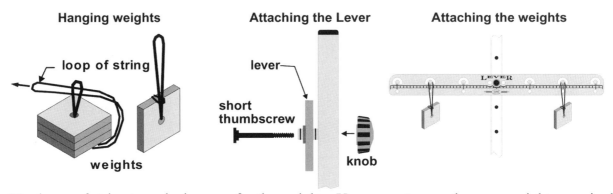

1   Use loops of string to make hangers for the weights. You can put more than one weight on a single string.
2   The weights can be hung from the lever by hooking the string over the center peg in the holes. Make sure that the string is all the way around the peg!

2 ## Levers in equilibrium

a.   The lever is in equilibrium when all the weights on one side balance all the weights on the other side. Hang the weights as shown below. Does the lever balance?
b.   What variables can be changed to balance a lever?

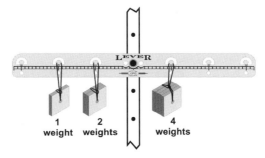

3   Trying different combinations to balance the lever

Make different combinations of weights and positions that balance. Use the chart below to write down the numbers of weights you put in each position. If you want to conduct more than four trials, write your results on a separate sheet of paper

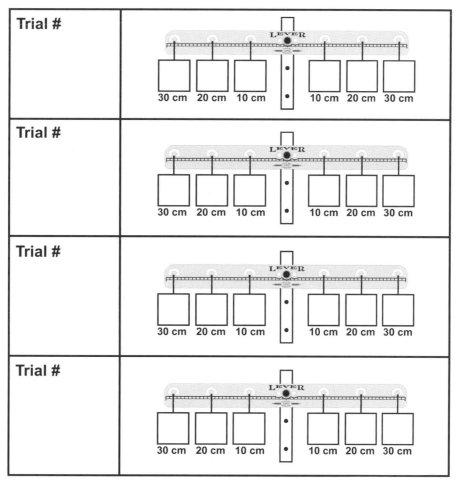

4   Determine the mathematical rule for equilibrium

Using the data in the chart above, determine a mathematical rule for levers in equilibrium. Think about the variables in the experiment: input force, output force, length of input arm, and length of output arm. Use your lab notebook to make calculations, then write your rule as an equation.

5   What did you learn?

a. Draw a lever that has mechanical advantage in your lab notebook. Label these parts: fulcrum, input arm, output arm, input force, and output force.

b. There are two ratios that can be used to determine mechanical advantage in levers. What are the two equations? What is the relationship between the two equations?

c. In a lever, you can increase the amount of output force by increasing the length of the input arm. When you do this, what must decrease in order to increase output force?

4.3 Designing Gear Machines

Question: How do gears work?

In this Investigation, you will:

1   Build machines with gears and deduce the rule for how pairs of gears turn.
2   Apply ratios to design machines with gears.
3   Design a gear machine to solve a specific problem.

Many machines require that rotating motion be transmitted from one place to another. The transmission of rotating motion is often done with shafts and gears. When one or more shafts are connected with gears, the shafts may turn at different speeds and in different directions. Since they act like rotating levers, gears also allow the forces carried by different shafts to be changed.

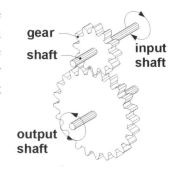

1   Two gear machines

1   Set up machines with two gears with different numbers of teeth as shown in the diagram.
2   Count the number of turns of the input gear it takes to make a whole number of turns of the output gear (such as one or two full turns). Write the data in the table below.

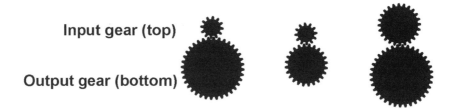

Input gear (top)

Output gear (bottom)

Table 1: Teeth and turns for 3 gear machines

Input Teeth	Input Turns	Output Teeth	Output Turns

2   Deducing the rule for gears

From your data, derive a mathematical formula which relates the turns of the input gear to the turns of the output gear. The rule also must include the teeth in each gear. State your rule using four variables: Input Teeth, Input Turns, Output Teeth, and Output Turns. This rule is called the *law of gearing* and is the basis for designing machines that use gears.

3   Complex gear machines

Many machines require large gear ratios. For example, a clock has a gear ratio of 1:60 between the minute hand and the second hand. This ratio could be made with one pair of gears where one gear was 60 times larger than the other. It can also be done with two pairs of gears in a much smaller and more economical design.

1   Set up a compound gear machine with at least 2 pairs of gears.

2   Use the table to work out the gear ratio.

3   Measure the rotation of the input and output gears and show that the machine behaves as you expect.

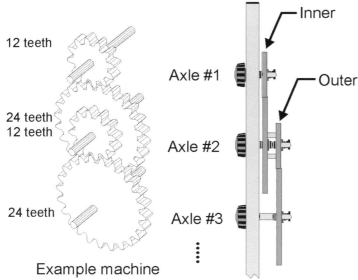

Example machine

Table 2: Gear machine #1

axle	Inner Position X or number of teeth	Outer Position X or number of teeth
1		
2		
3		
4		
5		

4   Design your own machine

The gears make ratios containing the numbers 1, 2, and 3 only. These ratios can be combined to make other ratios as long as no factors other than 1, 2, or 3 are used. It would be impossible to build a ratio of 21 with these gears because 21 factors into 7×3. You do not have any gears that can make a ratio of 7.

1   Design and construct a machine that has a ratio of 9:1. Make a table like the one above to record the design and show that the ratio works out mathematically.

2   Design and construct a machine that has a ratio of 4:1. Make a table like the one above to record the design and show that the ratio works out mathematically.

3   Design and construct a machine that has a ratio of 18:1. Make a table like the one above to record the design and show that the ratio works out mathematically. This ratio may require sharing with other groups since it uses at least 6 gears.

5   What did you learn?

a.   Suppose you needed to make a ratio of 100:1 using gears. Suggest 3 different designs using 3 different combinations of gears. Which design is the smallest? Which has the least gears?

b.   Are there reasons you might want to use two pairs of gears instead of 1 pair, even for small ratios? Think about the direction the input and output gears turn.

5.1 Work

Question: What happens when you multiply forces in a machine?

In this Investigation, you will:

1 Explore how simple machines are able to multiply forces.
2 Calculate work.

In Investigations 4.1 and 4.2, you learned how two simple machines can be arranged to provide a mechanical advantage. Ropes and pulleys, as do levers, create large output forces from small input forces. In this Investigation you will explore the nature of work and energy and come to an interesting conclusion that is true for all machines.

1 Setting up the experiment

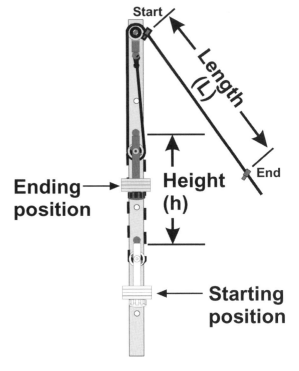

a. Using a ropes and pulleys set, clip the end of the yellow string to the bottom block. Pass the string over the middle pulley of the top block.

b. Use the marker stop (cord stop) to mark where the string leaves the top pulley.

c. Lift the bottom block a fixed height (h). The holes in the stand are 5 centimeters apart and you can use the holes as a height reference. Use at least 20 centimeters as your lifting height.

d. Measure how much string length (L) you had to pull to lift the block the chosen distance. You can measure this using the marker stops and a ruler.

e. Using the force scale, measure the force needed to lift the block. This is the **input force**.

f. Record the input force, height difference for the block (h), and string length (L) in the data table on the next page.

g. Leave the last two columns on the table blank for now.

h. Rearrange the yellow strings so that you achieve a mechanical advantage of 2, 3, 4, 5, and 6. For each combination record the height (h), input force, and string length (L) you had to pull to raise the block the required height (h).

Nature does not give things away for free. You traded something away to get the multiplication of forces.

i. As the mechanical advantage increases, what happens to the length of the string you have to pull to raise the block?

2   Data table

Mechanical advantage	Height difference for block	String length	Input force	Output force (weight of block)	Work done on block (work output)	Work done by you (work input)
	(meters)	(meters)	(newtons)	(newtons)	(joules)	(joules)

3   What is work?

The last two columns of the data table show the work done on the block and the work done by you. To do work, forces are applied to move objects. Simple machines like the block and tackle have mechanical advantage so that you can do work using less force.

To analyze how work and force are related, a specific definition for work is needed:

Work is the product of force times the distance moved in the direction of the force.

The units of work are newtons × meters (force × distance). The unit newton-meter was given the special name joule after Sir James Joule, who discovered the importance of work in a series of experiments performed between 1843 and 1847.

1 joule = 1 newton × 1 meter

4   Calculating work done

a. Calculate the work done on the block. This work is equal to the output force (weight of the block) times the height difference for block. The work done on the block should be the same for all configurations of the strings because the weight of the block and the height it was lifted did not change. You should therefore write the same number in each row of the table under the heading "Work done on block."

b. Next, calculate the work you did as you pulled on the string to lift the block. In this case, multiply the input force times the string length. For each different mechanical advantage, record the work done on the string under the heading "Work done by you."

5   ## The relationship between work and energy

Suppose that you use the block and tackle to lift the block 0.5 meter. If the weight of the block is 10 newtons, the amount of work done on the block is 0.5 m × 10 N = 5 joules. Where does this work go?

When work is done against gravity, it is not necessarily gone, but can be stored for future use. For example, suppose you lift marble A with a pulley as in the picture below.

a. Marble A can be let back down to lift marble B. The work put into lifting marble A can be recovered and used to lift marble B. Study the picture below carefully. In order for marble A to lift marble B, what must be true about the weights of the two marbles?

b. Using the arrows in the picture below as a guide, describe the forces in terms of strength and direction on marble A and marble B.

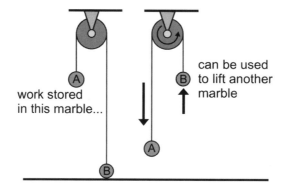

c. The work that is stored up when the first marble is lifted is a type of **energy**. Do you think the work being used to lift the second marble is the same, or a different type of energy? Explain.

d. When 10 joules is used to lift the block on the ropes and pulleys set, this work is stored up as energy. If we let the block back down again, we can get the energy back. You can confirm this by noticing that the string is pulling on you as you let the block fall back down. Try this out and explain your results in terms of work and energy.

6 The work-energy theorem

An object that has energy has the ability to do work. The total amount of work that can be done is exactly equal to the energy available. This principle is called the **work-energy theorem** and applies to everything in the universe.

a. Can you think of one everyday example that demonstrates the work-energy theorem?

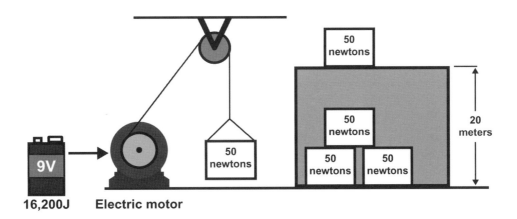

b. One way to store energy is in a battery. One 9-volt alkaline battery stores approximately 16,200 joules of energy. Suppose you had a perfect electric motor and a pulley with no friction. How many 50-newton boxes can you lift to a height of 20 meters using the energy stored in the battery? Solve the problem and show your work.

Energy Conservation

Question: What is energy and how does it behave?

In this Investigation, you will:

1   Discover the relationship between speed and height on a roller coaster.

2   Describe how energy is conserved on a roller coaster.

To pedal your bike up a hill, you have to work hard to keep the bike going. However, when you start down the other side of the hill, you coast! You hardly have to pedal at all. In this Investigation, you will find out what happens to the speed of a marble as it rolls up and down the hills and valleys of the CPO roller coaster.

1   Setting up the roller coaster

Attach the roller coaster to the fifth hole from the bottom of the stand. Use the starting peg to start the marble in the same place each time you roll it down. It sometimes takes a few tries to roll it straight so that it stays on the track. Watch the marble roll along the track. At which place (or places) do you think the marble moves fastest? Why?

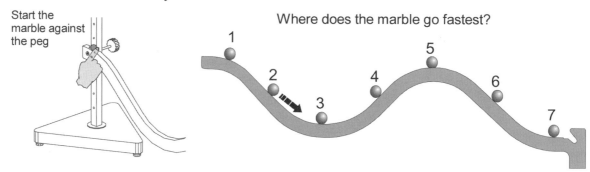

2   Measuring the speed of the marble

To understand what is happening to the marble, you need to measure the speed and the height at different places on the roller coaster.

1   To measure the speed of the marble, attach a photogate so that the marble breaks the light beam as it rolls through.

2   Plug the photogate into input A of the timer and use interval mode.

3   Be sure that the bottom of the photogate is flat against the bottom of the roller coaster. If the photogate is not attached properly, the light beam will not cross the center of the marble and the speed you calculate will not be accurate.

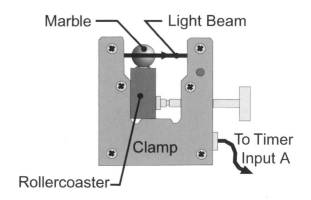

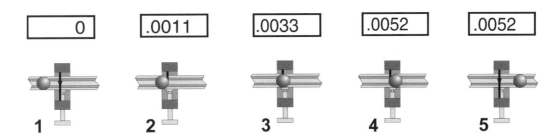

0	.0011	.0033	.0052	.0052
1	**2**	**3**	**4**	**5**

1   The ball has not broken the beam yet. The timer is not counting.

2   The timer starts counting when the front edge of the marble breaks the beam.

3   The timer keeps counting while the beam is blocked by the marble.

4   The timer stops counting when the back edge of the marble goes out of the beam.

5   The display shows the time that the marble blocked the beam.

Speed is the distance traveled divided by time taken to travel that distance. During the time that the timer is counting, the marble moves one diameter. Therefore, the distance traveled is the diameter of the marble, and the time taken is the time from photogate A. **The speed of the marble is its diameter divided by the time from photogate A.**

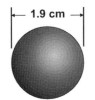

⟵ 1.9 cm ⟶

Use the photogate to test your hypothesis about where the marble would go fastest. Measure and record the speed of the marble at each of the seven places. Positions 2, 4, and 6 should be as close to the same height as you can get. If they are the same height, you can easily compare uphill and downhill motion.

Position number	Time, photogate A (sec)	Distance traveled (cm)	Speed of marble (cm/sec)
1			
2			
3			
4			
5			
6			
7			

a.   Did your measurements agree with your hypothesis or did they point to a different hypothesis? If the answer did not agree with your hypothesis, what sort of hypothesis do the observations support about where the marble is fastest?

b.   What did you notice about the motion of the marble from the measurements? For example, do you think that going uphill or downhill makes a difference in the speed? Does height affect speed? Which has a larger impact, height or direction (uphill or downhill)?

3 Energy conservation

When the marble speeds up, it is gaining kinetic energy from falling down a hill. The kinetic energy is converted from the potential energy the marble had at the top of the hill. As the marble goes along it trades potential and kinetic energy back and forth.

To measure the kinetic energy, we use the photogate to find the speed of the marble. To get the potential energy, we need to measure the height. The light beam passes through the center of the marble, so you should measure the height from the table to the center of the hole for the light beam.

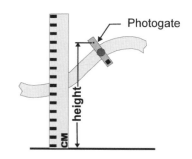

For the positions close to the start, you will have to measure from the base of the stand. Add the height of the base to the height you measure to get the total height.

1   Place the photogate at different places along the roller coaster.
    Measure the speed and height of the marble at each place.

2   Write your data down in the table below

Position (cm)	Height (cm)	Time from photogate A (sec)	Distance traveled (cm)	Speed of marble (cm/sec)
			1.9	
			1.9	
			1.9	
			1.9	
			1.9	
			1.9	
			1.9	
			1.9	
			1.9	
			1.9	
			1.9	
			1.9	

4   Graphing height vs. speed

Take your measurements and make a graph that shows the relationship between height and speed. The graph provided already shows the height of the roller coaster plotted against the position along the track. Plot the speed vs. position on the same graph.

Height and Speed vs. Position

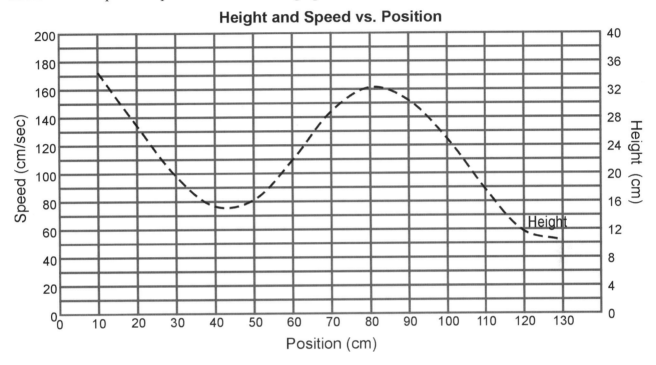

a.   What can you tell from your graph? Describe the relationship you see between the speed of the marble and the height.

b.   Where is the speed of the marble greatest?

c.   Does the uphill or downhill direction matter to the speed of the marble, or is the height the only contributing variable?

d.   Describe the flow of energy between potential and kinetic along the roller coaster. Your answer should indicate where the potential energy is greatest and least, and also where the kinetic energy is greatest and least.

5.3

Energy Transformations

Question: Where did the energy go?

In this Investigation, you will:

1 Describe energy transformations in several scenarios.

You have learned that the amount of energy in the universe is constant and that in any situation requiring energy, all of it must be accounted for. This is the basis for the law of conservation of energy. In this Investigation, you will analyze different scenarios in terms of what happens to energy. Based on your experience with the roller coaster, you already know that potential energy can be changed into kinetic energy and vice versa. As you study the scenarios below, identify potential energy to kinetic energy transformations. For each scenario, see if you can also answer the following questions: What other energy transformations are occurring? In each scenario, where did all the energy go?

1 ## Kinetic to potential, or potential to kinetic?

For each scenario, specify whether kinetic energy is being changed to potential energy, or potential is being converted to kinetic. Explain your answers.

a. A roller coaster car travels from point A to point B.

b. A bungee cord begins to exert an upward force on a falling bungee jumper.

c. A football is spiraling downward toward a football player.

d. A solar cell is charging a battery.

2 Energy scenarios

Read each scenario below. Then, working with your group, complete the following for each scenario:

- Identify the types of energy involved.

- Identify where potential energy is being converted to kinetic energy or kinetic to potential.

- Make an energy flow chart that shows the energy transformations that are occurring. Use a separate paper (newsprint, if provided) and colored markers to make your flow charts more interesting.

Be prepared to explain to the rest of the class the reasoning behind your group's ideas, and then to discuss them.

Scenario 1:

In Western states, many homes generate electricity from windmills. In a particular home, a young boy is using the electricity to run a toy electric train.

Scenario 2:

A woman is driving home from work. She is listening to the radio and singing her favorite song

Scenario 3:

The state of Illinois generates most of its electricity from nuclear power. A young woman in Chicago is watching a sports game on television.

Scenario 4:

A bicyclist is riding at night. He switches on his bike's generator so that his headlight comes on. The harder he pedals, the brighter his headlight glows.

6.1

Question: What is an electric circuit?

In this Investigation, you will:

1   Construct simple electric circuits using a battery, bulb, switch, and wires.
2   Draw circuit diagrams using electrical symbols.

Electricity is an integral part of our lives. Our homes, stores, and workplaces all use many electrical devices such as electric ovens, TVs, stereos, toasters, motors that turn fans, air conditioners, heaters, light bulbs, etc. In fact, the use of electricity has become so routine that many of us don't stop to think about what happens when we switch on a light or turn on a motor. If we do stop to look, we find that most of what is "happening" is not visible. What exactly is electricity? How does it work?

In this Investigation, you will figure out how to make a bulb light. As you build circuits, you will discover that electricity travels through a specific path, much like water travels through pipes or streams.

Safety Tips: Be careful working with batteries. If they are damaged or broken, return them immediately to your teacher.

If a battery or wire gets hot, disconnect the circuit and ask your teacher for help.

Always have a bulb somewhere in your circuit. Do not connect a wire directly from one terminal of the battery to the other terminal. This is a short circuit, which can start a fire.

1

Building circuits with a battery, a bulb, and a wire

a.   Using *only* one battery, one bulb, and one wire, find four different ways you can arrange these three parts that will make the bulb light up. As you work, determine the kinds of connections that are needed to make the circuit work.

b.   Record all your circuit attempts in your lab notebook. Draw both successful and unsuccessful attempts. The drawing at right shows a simple way to draw the bulb, battery and wire.

c.   Make sure your drawings show the difference between the two ends of the battery. Also show exactly where the bulb is touching the wire and the battery.

d.   In your lab notebook, explain why you think some configurations work and others don't. Record your first thoughts and impressions — don't worry if your answers are right or wrong.

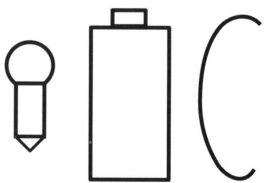

Using simple geometric shapes (circle, rectangle, triangle) and a line, you can draw representations of the light bulb, battery and wire.

2   ## Using the electricity grid

In this part of the Investigation, you will build the same circuit you made in part 1, except you will now use the electricity grid. The grid contains battery holders and light bulb holders, which makes building circuits a lot easier. Your completed circuit should include one battery and battery holder, one bulb and bulb holder, and two wire connectors. The bulb should light up in the completed circuit.

3   ## Drawing circuit diagrams

a. It was pretty difficult drawing the battery and bulb and wire in part 1! People who work with electricity have short-cut methods for drawing electrical parts and circuits. All the electrical parts in a circuit are represented by standard pictures, called *electrical symbols*. Some electrical parts and their corresponding symbols are shown in the picture to the right. Study the symbols and practice drawing them.

b.   Using these symbols, draw a picture of the circuit you built on the electricity grid. This type of drawing is called a *circuit diagram*. There is an example of a circuit diagram in your book on page 99.

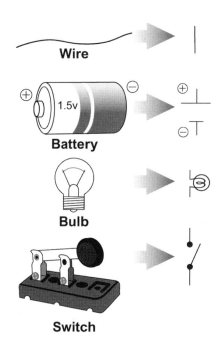

Wire

Battery

Bulb

Switch

4   ## Observing how a switch works

a. Add a switch to your circuit. You may need one more wire connector.

b. Check that the switch turns the light bulb on and off.

c. Examine the switch as it turns the light bulb on and off. In your lab notebook, explain how the switch works. Use both words and drawings.

5   ## What did you learn?

a. Water can travel through air but cannot travel through a solid. Using what you learned in this Investigation, describe some materials that electricity can and cannot travel through.

b. The word "circuit" comes from the same root as the word "circle." Describe the similarities between a circle and the circuits that you built.

c. A circuit that is on and working is sometimes called a "closed circuit." Based on your observations of the switch, explain what "closed" means in a circuit.

d. A circuit that is off or a circuit that is not working is sometimes called an "open circuit." Based on your observations of the switch, explain what "open" means in a circuit.

Charge

Question: What is moving through a circuit?

In this Investigation, you will:

1 Build a simple electroscope.
2 Charge pieces of tape.
3 Observe the electrostatic forces exerted by charged pieces of tape on each other.

To understand electricity, people studied events like lightning and the sparks that occur when certain materials are rubbed together. We now know that the movement of electric charge causes these events. Charge is a concept somewhat difficult to grasp; we see its manifestations around us but we can't "see" charge. In this way, charge is like the wind — we can't see the moving air but we know it exists because it blows against our faces and moves objects around.

Charge comes in two forms, called positive charge and negative charge. In this Investigation you will observe how these two kinds of charge interact with each other.

1 Building a simple electroscope

1 Obtain the following materials: two rectangles of clay about 2 cm by 2 cm by 4 cm, 4 flexible straws, ruler, and Scotch™ brand magic tape.

2 Anchor a flexible straw in each end of each piece of clay. You have 2 clay bases and 4 straws in all.

3 Bend the flexible straws away from each other in each piece of clay. The bent part is called the arm. The arms should be at the same height.

4 Line up the two pieces of clay so that the arms are parallel to each other and about 16 cm apart.

2 Creating static charges (a)

a. Place a piece of tape, about 20 cm long, sticky side down, on your table. This is your "base tape." It will always stay on the table.

b. Tear off a15-cm long piece of tape and turn over about 1/2 cm at the end to make a handle.

c. Place this piece of tape, sticky side down, on the base tape. Smooth the tape down.

d. Quickly tear away the handled tape and wrap the top part of it around one of the electroscope arms. Most of the tape should be dangling.

e. Repeat steps 2 through 5, only this time, place the second piece of tape on an arm on the second piece of clay. (You should still have two free arms on your electroscope.)

3 Observing the interaction between the tapes (a)

a. Line up the two electroscope halves so that the two pieces of tape are parallel to each other. Slowly move the two pieces of clay towards each other.

b. Observe and record what happens to the two pieces of tape.

4   Creating static charges (b)

1 Separate the two pieces of clay so that they are once again about 16 cm apart. Position them so that the two free arms are parallel to each other.

2 Tear off a 15-cm long piece of tape and turn over about 1/2 cm at the end to make a handle.

3 Place this piece of tape, sticky side down, on the base tape.

4 Label the handle A.

5 Tear off another 15-cm long piece of tape and again make a handle.

6 Place this piece of tape, sticky side down, on the A tape, which is still atop the base tape.

7 Label the handle of this second piece of tape B.

8 Remove the A and B tapes keeping them stuck together.

9 While holding them in the air, quickly tear apart the A and B tapes.

10 Place the A tape on one free arm of the electroscope.

11 Place the B tape on the last free arm of the electroscope.

5   Observing the interaction between the tapes (b)

a. Line up the two electroscope halves so that A and B pieces of tape are parallel to each other. Slowly move the two pieces of clay towards each other.

b. Observe and record what happens to the two pieces of tape.

c. Now see how the A and B tapes interact with the first two pieces of tape you prepared. Record what you observe.

6   What did you learn?

a. How many types of interactions did you observe between the pieces of tape?

b. The first tapes you prepared pushed each other away, or *repelled* each other. These two pieces of tape have the same kind of charge. This makes sense since you prepared the tapes in the same way. On the other hand, the A tape has one kind of charge and the B tape has a different kind of charge. Are the first tapes you prepared both A tapes or both B tapes? Explain how you figured this out.

c. Give your hypothesis for how the A and B tapes might have acquired different kinds of charge.

7   ☒ Extension: Using the electroscope to detect other charged objects

In sixteenth-century England, William Gilbert, the queen's physician, built the first electroscope. He noticed that the electroscope attracted lightweight objects. See if you can reproduce his results.

1 Remove the tape from your electroscope

2 Prepare and label a fresh set of A and B tapes and place them on two arms anchored in one piece of clay.

3 Take light objects such as thread, small pieces of paper, and hair and slowly bring them close to both the A and B tapes.

4 Record your observations.

Voltage

Question: Why do charges move through a circuit?

In this Investigation, you will:

1   Measure the voltage of a battery with an electrical meter.

2   Measure the voltage of batteries in and out of circuits.

3   Figure out how batteries must be connected together in order to increase voltage in a circuit.

Have you ever wondered how a battery works? Or what "volts" mean?

You know that batteries have one end marked positive and one end marked negative. A battery supplies energy to create electric current that flows from positive to negative. The energy you supplied by raising and lowering the string with the ropes and pulleys could do work. In a similar way, the electric current that flows through a wire can also do work. *Voltage* describes how much energy is available to make electric current flow and do work. The higher the voltage, the more current will flow and do work for us. The work includes lighting bulbs, heating toast, and turning electric motors.

◆ **Safety Tips: Be careful working with batteries. If they are damaged or broken, return them immediately to your teacher.**

If a battery or wire gets hot, disconnect the circuit and ask your teacher for help.

Always have a bulb somewhere in your circuit. Do not connect a wire directly from one terminal of the battery to the other terminal. This is a short circuit, which can start a fire.

1   Measuring voltage across a battery

1   Gather the following materials: electrical meter and its two test leads, and a battery.

2   Connect the two meter leads to the meter as shown in the bottom of the picture at right.

3   Set the meter to measure DC volts.

4   Place the red positive lead of the meter on the positive terminal of the battery.

5   Place the black negative lead of the meter on the negative terminal of the battery.

6   Look at the voltage reading. If the number is not close to 1.5 volts or if the range needs to be adjusted, ask your teacher for help.

7   Record the voltage of the battery.

2 Measure voltage across a battery in a circuit

1   Gather the following additional materials: a battery holder, a bulb, a bulb holder, and two connectors.

2   Build a circuit with the battery you just tested, a battery holder, a bulb, a bulb holder, and two connectors.

3   Predict what the voltage of the battery will be while it is lighting the bulb. Also explain the reasoning behind your prediction.

4   Measure the voltage across the battery exactly as you did in part 1. DO NOT DISCONNECT THE CIRCUIT.

5   Record the voltage of the battery while it is lighting the bulb.

3 What did you learn?

a.   Was your prediction correct?

b.   Was there much difference in the battery voltage when it was not lighting the bulb and when it was lighting the bulb?

c.   A battery has chemicals inside that react with each other and release energy. This energy separates and moves the charges to each terminal of the battery. Draw a picture that shows this process taking place inside a battery.

4 Building circuits with two batteries

How many batteries does a small flashlight use? How about a large radio? What happens when you wire batteries together?

Build circuits with two batteries, two battery holders, one bulb, one bulb holder, and three wires. Connect the two batteries in four different configurations as shown.

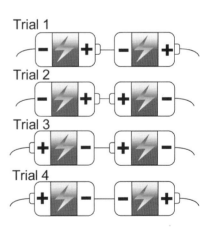

1   For each configuration, do the following:

2   Record if the bulb lights.

3   Predict what the voltage will be across the bulb.

4   Measure voltage across the two bulbs.

Not every combination will light the bulb.

a.   Which configurations light the bulb? Describe in words how you should wire batteries together.

b.   Examine your data. Each battery is 1.5 volts. Explain the rule for how to calculate voltage when 2 batteries are connected correctly.

c.   What happens to the energy of the charges in a circuit when batteries are wired together? Discuss this question with your group and record your answer.

Current

Question: How does current move through a circuit?

In this Investigation, you will:

1 Measure and compare current at different points in a circuit.

2 Compare current in circuits with one and two bulbs.

Why does a bulb light? When you put a battery in a circuit, electric current flows through the wires and makes things happen. The current carries energy from the battery to a bulb or motor. You can increase the amount of energy in two ways. The higher the flow of current, the more the energy that can be carried. The higher the voltage, the more energy can be carried by the same amount of current.

⬥Safety Tips: Be careful working with batteries. If they are damaged or broken, return them immediately to your teacher.

If a battery or wire gets hot, disconnect the circuit and ask your teacher for help.

1 Building test circuit #1

1 Gather the following materials: electrical meter and its two test leads, a battery and battery holder, a bulb and bulb holder, and two connectors.

2 Build test circuit 1 with one battery and battery holder, one bulb and bulb holder, and two connectors, as shown in the schematic at right. There are two points marked on the schematic, A and B, which is where the connectors are attached to the bulb holder. Make sure that you can easily identify these points in your circuit.

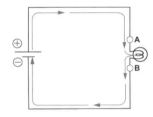

2 Measuring current through test circuit #1

To measure current, the meter must be placed *in* the circuit so the current has to flow through the meter. Follow the instructions below carefully.

1 Connect the two meter leads to the meter as shown right.

2 Set the meter to measure DC current at the highest range.

3 Remove the connector between the positive terminal of the battery and the bulb holder.

4 Place the red positive lead of the meter on the post attached to the positive terminal of the battery.

5 Place the black negative lead of the meter on the free post attached to the bulb holder. You should now have a complete circuit. The bulb should light and you should get a reading on the meter.

6 Record the current at point A.

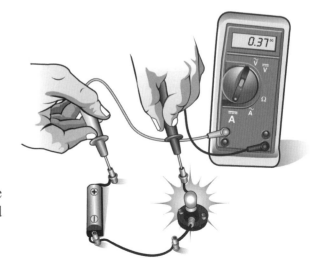

7   Predict what the current at point B will be. Record your prediction.

8   Following the same procedure you did for point A, use your meter to measure current at point B. The positive lead of the meter should be closest to the positive battery terminal, and the negative lead of the meter should be closest to the negative battery terminal.

9   Record the current at point B.

10 Remove the meter and reconnect the circuit. Leave it connected while you complete part 3.

3 Building test circuit #2

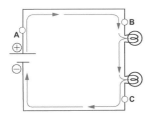

1 Gather the following additional materials: one battery and battery holder, two bulbs and bulb holders, and three connectors.

2 Build the circuit in the diagram on the left. Make sure that you can easily identify points A, B, and C where the connectors are attached.

4 Comparing test circuits #1 and #2

Compare the brightness of the bulbs in test circuits 1 and 2. Record your observations and disconnect test circuit 1.

5 Measuring current through test circuit #2

1   Using the same procedure you followed in part 2, measure and record current at point A.

2   Predict what the current will be at points B and C.

3   Using the same procedure you followed in part 2, measure and record current at points B and C.

6 What did you learn?

a.   Review the two current readings for circuit 1. What conclusions can you draw from these results?

b.   Review the three current readings for circuit 2. What conclusions can you draw from these results?

c.   Transfer all your results for circuit 1 and circuit 2 into the table below. Compare the current readings in the two circuits. What happened to current when you added a bulb to the circuit?

	Current in circuit 1 (amps)		Current in circuit 2 (amps)
point A		point A	
point B		point B	
		point C	

d.   You probably determined that adding a bulb to the circuit reduced the current. With the rest of your group propose an explanation. Be prepared to present and defend your explanation.

Resistance

Question: How well does current travel through different materials and objects?

In this Investigation, you will:

1 Determine how different objects differ in their ability to resist current.
2 Classify materials as conductors, insulators, or semiconductors.
3 Compare the resistance of identical pieces of copper and aluminum wires.
4 Determine how electrical resistance varies with length.

Materials differ in their ability to allow current to flow through them. This is a good thing! It means that we can build circuits out of metals that easily carry current. We can block the flow of current using air, glass, or plastic. *Resistance* is the quantity that describes how much an object will prevent (resist) the flow of current. Resistance is measured in a unit called ohms.

1   **Measuring resistance of everyday objects**

1 Gather the following materials: electrical meter and its two test leads, and resistance test objects.

1 Examine the objects and try to determine what material each is made out of. Include air as one of your test objects. You can ask your teacher for assistance. Record your answers in Table 1.

2 Connect the two meter leads to the meter as shown at right.

3 Set the meter to measure resistance.

4 Measure the resistance of each object. To do this, attach the black negative meter lead to one end of the test object and then attach the red positive meter lead to the other end of the test object. (Use your ruler to measure the resistance of 1 centimeter of air.)

5 Some materials may have a high resistance and the meter will read OL. Record these readings as "very high." Record all resistances in Table 1.

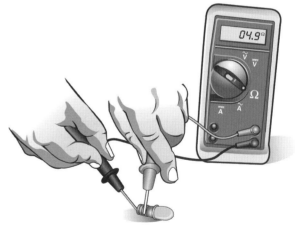

Table 1: Resistance of common objects

Object	Material, if known	Resistance in ohms	Object	Material, if known	Resistance in ohms

2   Identifying conductors and insulators

To roughly describe the ability of different kinds of materials to conduct current, we say that a material is a conductor (conducts easily), an insulator (conducts poorly), or a semiconductor (in-between). All of these materials are useful when we construct circuits.

Table 2: Classifying materials as conductors, insulators, or semiconductors

Object / material listed from low to high resistance	Resistance in ohms (from Table 1)	Conductor, insulator, or semiconductor	Was your classification correct?

1   Rearrange the list of objects you tested (in Table 1) so that the readings of resistance go from lowest to highest. Copy your rearranged list of objects and their resistance into Table 2.

2   Look at your results and try to classify the objects you tested under one of these three categories: conductors, insulators, and semiconductors. As a guideline, remember that bulbs and wires are conductors and air is an insulator. (Hint: It is likely that only one item on your list is a semiconductor.) Write down your classifications in column 3.

3   Check your results against the table on page 118 of your book. How well did you do? Record whether or not your classification was correct in column 4.

3   Measuring and comparing resistance of copper and aluminum

a.   Your teacher will give you two identical wires of aluminum and copper. Which metal do you think will have more resistance? Why?

b.   Measure the resistance of both pieces of metal. You can bend the wire so that the meter leads can reach the ends. Record your results.

c.   Which metal has the lowest resistance? Do you know if this metal is commonly used in electric circuits?

d.   Fold each piece of wire neatly in half and mark the halfway point. Unfold the wire and measure resistance from the halfway point to one end of the wire. Record your results for copper and aluminum.

e.   Compare the resistance for the whole piece of each metal with the half piece. How does resistance vary with length?

f.   How do you think resistance of a wide wire will compare with that of a thin wire of the same length? Discuss this question with your group and record your answer. Think about the flow of water through narrow and wide pipes.

8.1

Ohm's Law

Question: How are voltage, current, and resistance related?

In this Investigation, you will:

1   Build circuits using resistors.

2   Measure change in current when resistance is changed.

3   Measure and graph change in current when voltage is changed.

4   Use your data and graph to determine the relationship between voltage, current, and resistance.

When working with circuits, there are many times when you want to know how much voltage will light a particular light bulb, or how much current will be in a circuit so you can choose the correct size wire to use. German physicist Georg S. Ohm (1787-1854) experimented with circuits to find out how voltage, current, and resistance are related mathematically. The relationship he discovered is called **Ohm's law**.

1   How does changing resistance affect current?

In this Investigation you will use electrical parts called *resistors*. They have a relatively constant resistance under different operating conditions and are widely used in circuits.

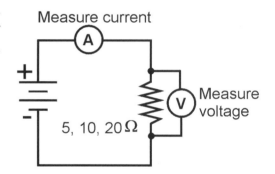

1   Gather the following materials: Electrical meter and test leads, two batteries and holders, a 5-ohm resistor, a 10-ohm resistor, a 20-ohm resistor, and three connectors.

2   Use the electrical meter to measure the resistance of the 5-ohm resistor. Record the value in Table 1.

3   Build the circuit shown in the schematic at right. Measure the voltage across the two batteries and record the value in Table 1.

4   Measure current through the circuit and record the value in your Table 1.

5   Remove the 5-ohm resistor and replace it with the10-ohm resistor, and 20 ohm resistor. Repeat steps 2-4 for each resistor. Record all measurements in Table 1.

Table 1: Change in current vs. change in resistance

	voltage (volts)	resistance (ohms)	current (amps)
Circuit with 5-ohm resistor			
Circuit with 10-ohm resistor			
Circuit with 20-ohm resistor			

a.   Examine your data. Is the resistance of each resistor exactly as labeled or is there some variation?

b.   Examine your data. Describe in words what happens to current as resistance is increased

2   How does changing voltage affect current?

1   Gather the following extra materials: one battery and holder and a resistor (5, 10, or 20 ohms).

2   Use the electrical meter to measure the resistance of the resistor you chose. Record the value in the first column, all three rows, of Table 2.

3   Build a circuit with one battery, your resistor, and the potentiometer as shown in the diagram at right.

4   Measure the voltage across the resistor, and the current through the circuit. Record the value in Table 2.

5   Change the setting of the potentiometer and measure voltage and current again. Repeat for at least 5 settings of the potentiometer. Record all values for voltage and current in the table.

6   Change the number of batteries, measure voltage and current again for a few settings of the potentiometer and record the results.

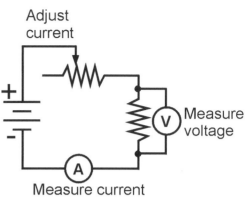

Adjust current

Measure voltage

Measure current

Table 2: Change in current vs. change in voltage

resistance (ohms)	voltage (volts)	current (amps)	resistance (ohms)	voltage (volts)	current (amps)

a. Examine the data in your table. Describe in words what happens to the voltage across the resistor as the current increases.

3   Finding the relationship between voltage, current, and resistance

a.   Graph the data from part 2. Put the independent variable (voltage) on the *x*-axis and the dependent variable (current) on the *y*-axis. Label your *x*- and *y*-axes and title your graph.

b.   The slope of a line is rise over run. For the graph of voltage vs. current, slope is change in voltage (rise) over change in current (run). Calculate the slope of the graph. What other electrical quantity in the circuit does the slope approximately equal?

c.   You just found out that the slope of the voltage vs. current graph is the resistance. This is the equation for Ohm's law. Write the mathematical equation for Ohm's law using the following: V stands for voltage, I stands for current, and R stands for resistance.

d.   Most circuits use fixed voltage sources. Different values of current are needed to run different devices and appliances. With this information, explain the importance of resistors in a circuit.

Work, Energy, and Power

Question: How much does it cost to use the electrical appliances in your home?

In this Investigation, you will:

1 Read appliance labels to determine their power rating.
2 Calculate the approximate number of kilowatt-hours each appliance uses in a month.
3 Calculate the approximate cost of running each appliance using electric company rates.

You have learned how to measure three electrical quantities: voltage, current, and resistance. In this Investigation, you will learn about a fourth quantity, power, which you have already studied in the context of mechanics. You will find the power ratings of electrical appliances and use this information to estimate electrical costs.

1 **Find the power rating of home appliances**

You will need to complete the first part of this Investigation at home. Your assignment is to find five electrical appliances that have a label with the device's power rating in watts or kilowatts. Some appliances you might investigate are a blender, coffee maker, toaster oven, microwave, television, hair dryer, space heater, room air conditioner, or an electric drill. The rating is often stamped on the back or the bottom of the appliance.

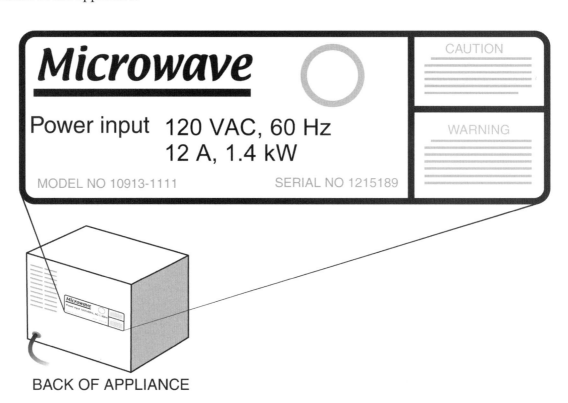

In the above example the power rating is 1.35 kW.

1   Fill out the first two columns of Table 1 as you find the power rating of each appliance. The second column should be in kilowatts.

2   Convert any power ratings listed in watts to kilowatts. To convert to kilowatts, divide the number of watts by 1,000. For example, 1500 watts is equal to $1500 \div 1000$, or 1.5 kilowatts. Fill in the kilowatt column for each device.

3   Finally, estimate the number of hours the device is used each month. Assume that one month equals 30 days. If your coffee maker is used for a half hour each morning, you would calculate one-half hour times 30 days equals 15 hours per month. You may need to talk to other people in your home to get the most accurate estimate possible.

4   After you have filled in the estimated monthly use column, you are ready to complete the rest of the Investigation in class.

Table 1: Power rating, usage, and cost of household appliances

Appliance	Power rating in kilowatts	Estimated hours per month in use	Number kWh per month	Price per kWh	Total cost per month
coffee maker	0.900	3.0	2.70		
coffee grinder	0.150	0.2	0.03		
microwave	1.000	10.0	10.0		
hairdryer	1.625				
VCR	0.020	20.0	0.40		

2   ## Estimate the number of kilowatt-hours each appliance uses in a month

In order to determine how much your household spends each month to use some of your appliances, you must first calculate the number of kilowatt-hours expended per month.

To do so, simply multiply the power rating in kilowatts (from the second column) by the number of hours the appliance is used each month. If you use a 1-kilowatt toaster for five hours a month, you would multiply 1 times 5.

Write your answers in column 4 of Table 1, as shown in the sample below.

Appliance	Power rating in kilowatts	Estimated hours per month in use	Number kWh per month	Price per kWh	Total cost per month
Microwave	1.35 kW	22 hours	29.7		

3   Determine the monthly cost of using your appliances

Utility companies charge consumers for the number of kilowatt-hours of electricity they use each month. Many houses and apartments have a meter attached to the outside of the building. The meter uses a system of spinning disks to record how much electricity you use. Someone from the electric company reads the meters once each month.

Find out how much you pay per kilowatt-hour (or kWh). In some areas, one utility company provides all the electricity to an entire region, while in another places, several electric companies compete for customers.

a. Research your area and write the price per kilowatt-hour in column 5 of Table 1.

b. Calculate the amount of money your household spends to operate each appliance during one month. Multiply the kilowatt-hours by the price per kilowatt-hour in order to determine your cost.

4   Analyze your data

a. Compare your results with those of the other members of your group. List the three appliances from your group that had the highest power ratings in Table 2.

b. Think about the function of each appliance listed above. What kind of work is being done? In other words, electrical energy is converted into what other type(s) of energy?

c. Do you see any similarities in the kinds of work being done by the three appliances in Table 2? If so, what are they?

d. Suggest one practical way you or another group member could reduce your electricity bills.

e. Discuss the effect of climate on electricity use. What climate factors might influence which month has the peak electrical use in your area?

f. Name one other factor (not related to climate) that may influence which month has the highest electricity use in your area.

Table 2: Appliances with the highest power ratings

Appliance	Power rating in kilowatts

5   What do you buy from the electric utility company?

People often use the phrase "power plant" to refer to their local electric company. You may have heard people say that electric companies "sell power" to their customers, or that there was a "power shortage" in a particular area. Let's take a look at these phrases from a scientific perspective. What, exactly, do electric companies sell?

We know that electricity bills charge for the number of kilowatt-hours (or kWh) used per month.

Let's first change kilowatt-hours to the units of watts and seconds:

$$1 \text{ kilowatt} \cdot \text{hour} \times \frac{1000 \text{ watts}}{\text{kilowatt}} = 1000 \text{ watt} \cdot \text{hours}$$

$$1000 \text{ watt} \cdot \text{hour} \times \frac{3600 \text{ seconds}}{\text{hour}} = 3,600,000 \text{ watt} \cdot \text{seconds}$$

(You may remember from previous study of fractions that a term appearing in both the numerator and denominator will cancel when the fractions are multiplied.)

Power is equal to the amount of work done per unit of time, or the amount of energy transferred in a circuit per unit of time. In specific units, a watt is equal to joules per second. We substitute the fundamental units of joules per second for watts.

$$3,600,000 \left(\frac{\text{joules}}{\text{second}} \right) \cdot \text{seconds} = ?$$

a.   Which terms in the last equation will cancel?

b.   After canceling the terms that appear in both the numerator and denominator, what is the fundamental unit that remains?

c.   Is the remaining unit a measure of energy, work, or power?

d.   Do electric companies sell energy, work, or power?

Types of Circuits

Question: What kinds of electric circuits can you build?

In this Investigation, you will:

1 Build and compare series and parallel circuits.

There are two different types of circuits, called series and parallel circuits. *Series circuits* have only one path for the flow of current. *Parallel circuits* have two or more paths for the flow of current. What does a simple circuit that rings a warning bell in your car have in common with the complex circuits that run computers? All circuits use series and parallel circuits, by themselves or combined with each other. In this Investigation, you will build these circuits and explore a common application of them.

◆**Safety Tips: Be careful working with batteries. If they are damaged or broken, return them immediately to your teacher.**

If a battery or wire gets hot, disconnect the circuit and ask your teacher for help.

Always have a bulb somewhere in your circuit. Do not connect a wire directly from one terminal of the battery to the other terminal or you will make a short circuit.

1 **Building two kinds of circuits**

1 Gather the following materials: two batteries and battery holders, two bulbs and bulb holders, and six connectors.

2 Build Circuit 1 pictured at right.

3 Trace the circuit path with a pencil from positive terminal to negative terminal. Does the current have any choice about where to go?

a) Describe the brightness of the two bulbs.

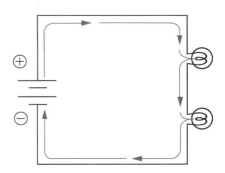

Circuit 1 (series circuit)

1 Build Circuit 2 pictured at right. The circuit "branches" at the square dots. If you are not sure how to build this configuration, ask your teacher for help.

2 Trace the circuit path with a pencil from positive terminal to negative terminal. Does the current have any choice about where to go?

b) Describe the brightness of the two bulbs.

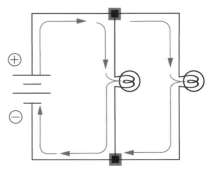

Circuit 2 (parallel circuit)

2 Analyzing your results

a. Compare the brightness of the bulbs in each kind of circuit. Which circuit has a greater transfer of energy?

b. Your household wiring is a parallel circuit, with each appliance or device on a separate branch of the circuit. With your group, discuss the possible advantages of using parallel circuits for a home. You can experiment with your parallel circuit to help you answer this question.

c. Write two paragraphs summarizing the points you discussed with your group, about the advantages of parallel circuits in the home.

3 An application of series and parallel circuits

Many circuits include multiple switches that are arranged in both series and parallel combinations. What is the purpose of these combinations?

If two switches are arranged in series, then both switches must be on for the circuit to work. This type of arrangement is called an **AND circuit**. If two switches are arranged in parallel, then only one switch needs to be on for the circuit to work. This type of arrangement is called an **OR circuit**.

Building an AND circuit

1 Gather the following materials: two switches and one connector. Build Circuit 3 pictured to the right.

2 Is this a series or parallel circuit?

3 Place a label next to each switch. Label one of the switches 1 and the other switch 2.

4 Try all combinations of switches: both on, both off, #1 on and #2 off, and #2 on and #1 off.

5 Record what happens to the bulb in each case.

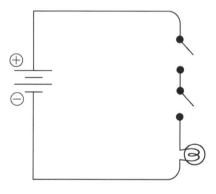

Circuit 3 (AND circuit)

Building an OR circuit

1 Build Circuit 4 pictured to the right.

2 Is this a series or parallel circuit?

3 Place a label next to each switch. Label one of the switches 1 and the other switch 2.

4 Try all combinations of switches: both on, both off, #1 on and #2 off, and #2 on and #1 off.

5 Record what happens to the bulb in each case.

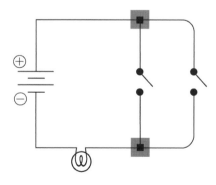

Circuit 4 (OR circuit)

a. A car will sound a warning bell if you open the door while the lights are on. Is this circuit an AND circuit or an OR circuit? Explain your reasoning.

Series Circuits

Question: How do you use Ohm's law in series circuits?

In this Investigation, you will:

1 Determine how to calculate total resistance in a series circuit.

2 Build a circuit with a dimmer switch.

◆Safety Tips: Be careful working with batteries. If they are damaged or broken, return them immediately to your teacher.

If a battery, resistor, or wire gets hot, disconnect the circuit and ask your teacher for help.

Always have a bulb or resistor somewhere in your circuit. Do not connect a wire directly from one terminal of the battery to the other terminal. This is a short circuit, which can start a fire.

1   Adding resistors in series circuits

1 Gather the following materials: Electrical meter and test leads, two batteries and battery holders, two 5-ohm resistors, one 10-ohm resistor, and five connectors.

2 Label the three resistors R1, R2, and R3. Measure the resistance of each and record the values in Table 1.

Table 1: Voltage and resistance values of your parts

R1 Resistance (ohms)	R2 Resistance (ohms)	R3 Resistance (ohms)	Battery voltage (volts)

3 Build circuit 1 as shown right. Use the R1 resistor.

4 Use the electrical meter to measure the voltage across both batteries. Record the value in Table 1.

5 Use the electrical meter to measure current through the circuit. Record the value in Table 2 on the next page.

6 Add the R2 resistor to the circuit. Your circuit has two resistors in total.

7 Measure current through the circuit. Record the value in Table 2.

8 Add the R3 resistor to the circuit. Your circuit has three resistors in total.

9 Measure current through the circuit. Record the value in Table 2.

10 Using Ohm's law (in the form $R = V/I$), calculate total resistance in each circuit, using the battery voltage (from Table 1) and the current for each circuit (from Table 2).

11 Record your results in Table 2.

Study your calculated resistances in Table 2. What is the rule for calculating total resistance in a series circuit, from individual resistances?

Table 2: Measurements of current when resistors are added in a circuit

	Circuit with R1	Circuit with R1, and R2	Circuit with R1, R2, and R3
Current in amps			
Resistance in ohms			

2　Building a circuit with a dimmer switch

Your circuit kit contains a *potentiometer*. A potentiometer is a variable resistor. As you turn the dial of the potentiometer, resistance goes up. Many of the dials you use everyday, like dimmer switches, are potentiometers.

Build a circuit with one battery, one bulb, and your potentiometer. Observe what happens when you turn the dial.

3　Finding the resistance of a bulb

If you measure the resistance of a bulb your value will not be very useful. This is because the resistance of a bulb varies a great deal depending on the amount of current through it. It *is* useful to know the resistance of your bulb at different values of current! You will find this information using the following procedure:

1　In your dimmer circuit, set the potentiometer to 0 ohms. Measure and record the battery voltage.

2　Measure current through the circuit. Record approximate bulb brightness and current in Table 3.

3　Repeat step 2 for all settings of the potentiometer. Record the current values in Table 3. Add more rows to the table as needed.

Table 3: Resistance of a bulb at different levels of current

Potentiometer resistance (ohms)	How bright is the bulb?	Battery voltage (volts)	Current (amps)	Bulb resistance (ohms)
0.0				
1.0				
2.0				
3.0				

Use the formula below (a version of Ohm's law) to calculate the resistance of the bulb at each potentiometer setting (R_{pot}). If you have time, see if you can figure out this formula on your own.

$$R_{bulb} = \frac{V_{battery}}{I} - R_{pot}$$

a.　Graph bulb resistance vs. current for each potentiometer setting. Label your axes and title your graph. Keep this graph for use in your next Investigation.

9.3 Parallel Circuits

Question: How do parallel circuits work?

In this Investigation, you will:

1 Build and analyze parallel circuits.

2 Determine how total current and branch currents are related in parallel circuits.

3 Apply your understanding of parallel circuits by building a test voltage circuit.

In the last Investigation, you learned how to use Ohm's law in series circuits. In this Investigation, you will build parallel circuits and measure their electrical quantities. Parallel circuits are complex and are not intuitive, so you will need to examine your data carefully to understand how these circuits work.

◆ Safety Tips: Be careful working with batteries. If they are damaged or broken, return them immediately to your teacher.

1 Measuring current and voltage in a parallel circuit

Series Circuit

1 Gather the following materials: Electrical meter and its test leads, two batteries and battery holders, two bulbs and bulb holders, and six connectors.

2 Using both batteries, build the series circuit shown right.

3 Measure current through the circuit and record it in the table below.

4 Measure and record the voltage drop across the bulb. Do this by placing the red positive meter lead on the positive side of the bulb holder and the black negative lead on the negative side of the bulb holder. (The circuit needs to be on.) Record the value in the table.

5 Calculate resistance using Ohm's law. Record it in the table.

Parallel Circuit

1 Using both batteries, build the parallel circuit shown at right. Measure current through branch 1 and branch 2. (The "A" symbol on the circuit diagram indicates where to measure current in each branch.) Record the values in the table below.

2 Measure and record the voltage drop across each bulb.

3 Using Ohm's law, calculate the resistance in each branch. Record the values in the table below.

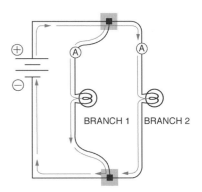

Series circuit		Parallel circuit	branch 1	branch 2
Current		Current		
Voltage drop		Voltage drop		
Resistance		Resistance		

2   What did you learn?

a.   Compare the current, voltage drops, and resistance in the series circuit with the parallel circuit.

b.   Your results should indicate that each branch of the parallel circuit is like another series circuit attached to the battery. As a result, the voltage drop is the same in all branches of a parallel circuit, and is equal to the voltage provided by the battery. What is happening in the battery as more parallel branches are added?

3   What is important about current values in parallel circuits?

a.   In parallel circuits, there is one part of the circuit path where all the charges flow through. This is where the current leaves and enters the battery terminals. In your parallel circuit, measure the total current at one of the battery terminals. Record your results.

b.   Compare the total current you just measured with the branch currents in the table above. What is the relationship between branch currents and total current in a parallel circuit?

4   Building a test voltage circuit

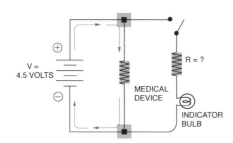

Portable electrical devices like radios and cell phones run on batteries. Usually, you only discover that the batteries are drained in these devices when they stop working. However, for some portable medical or industrial equipment, it is important to be able to anticipate when batteries need to be replaced. In this part of the Investigation, your challenge is to build a voltage test circuit that alerts you when battery voltage has dropped! A sample test voltage circuit is shown at left.

a.   Use one battery, one bulb, and your potentiometer to build the dimmer light circuit shown in the last Investigation. Slowly decrease resistance until the light bulb goes out. Measure and record the current though the circuit at this point.

b.   Study the test voltage circuit diagram above. What is the voltage drop across the second branch of the test voltage circuit?

c.   What will be the voltage drop if the total battery voltage drops to 80 percent of its original value?

d.   Use Ohm's law to calculate the total resistance needed in the second branch of the test voltage circuit. This is the resistance that will cause the bulb to go out at 80 percent of the battery voltage! Use the voltage value from step 4(c) and the current value from step 4(a) to calculate the total resistance needed in the second branch of the circuit.

e.   ![graph] Use the graph of bulb resistance vs. current from the last Investigation to figure out the bulb resistance at the current you measured in step 4(a).

f.   Calculate the unknown resistance shown in the test voltage circuit. You know the total resistance needed in the branch and the bulb resistance.

g.   Build the test voltage circuit. Use a 10-ohm resistor to represent the medical device.Use the potentiometer and set it to the resistance you just calculated in step 4(f). If your batteries are fully charged, the bulb should light when you turn on the switch!

h.   Your teacher will give you some used batteries. Label them and place them in your circuit. See if the light is off when you turn the switch!

10.1 **Permanent Magnets**

Question: What effects do magnets have?

In this Investigation, you will:

1   See how two magnets affect each other.
2   Measure the strength of the magnetic force.
3   Determine what kinds of materials are affected by magnets.
4   Determine if the magnetic force can be blocked by nonmagnetic materials.

In this Investigation, you will experiment with magnets in order to learn more about magnets and magnetic forces. The magnets you will use may not look like other magnets you've seen. The poles are on the opposite faces, as shown in the picture.

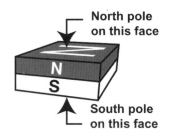

1   **Describing the forces that two magnets exert on each other**

a.   Try holding two magnets with their south poles facing each other. What happens?

b.   Try holding two magnets with their north poles facing each other. What happens?

c.   Try holding two magnets with north and south poles facing each other. What happens?

d.   Write down a rule that describes how magnets exert forces on each other. Your rule should take into account your observations from steps a-c, and should use at least two of the following words: attract, repel, north, south, and pole.

2 Determining how far the magnetic force reaches

How far does the magnetic force of a magnet reach? This is an important question for machines that use magnets.

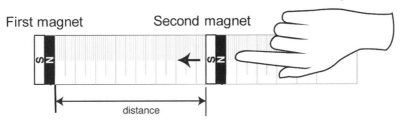

Move the second magnet closer and closer
until the field magnet first moves.

First magnet   Second magnet

distance

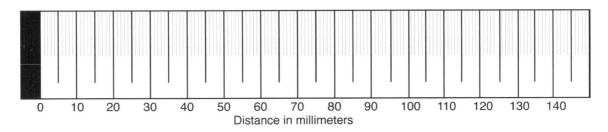

0   10   20   30   40   50   60   70   80   90   100   110   120   130   140
Distance in millimeters

1   Place one magnet on the solid rectangle on the ruler above and slide a second magnet closer and closer until the first magnet moves. Practice the technique several times before recording data.

2   In Table 1 below, record the distance between the magnets when you first see movement. Try each of the combinations of poles, north-north, south-south, and north-south.

3   For each combination do three tries, and average your three distances. (To get the average, add the three distances together and divide the total by 3.) Record the average in Table 1.

Look at your results and compare the distances for the three combinations of poles. Your answer should use the words *force* and *distance*.

Table 1: Magnetic forces between two magnets

	N-S	S-S	N-N
Distance 1			
Distance 2			
Distance 3			
Average distance			

3

Testing materials to see if they are affected by magnets

Not all materials are affected by magnetic forces. In this part of the Investigation you will see which materials respond to a magnet.

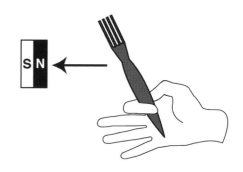

Use one of your magnets to try the set of materials your teacher will give you. You can try other materials in the classroom as well. See if each object is affected by the magnet. If it is, determine whether it is attracted to or repelled by the magnet. Record your data in Table 2 below.

Table 2: How different objects are affected by magnets

Object	Material composition	Attract	Repel	No effect

The word "magnetic" is used to describe things that are affected strongly by magnets. Look at your data table. How would you describe the things that are magnetic and the things that are not? Use the following words in your answer: magnetic and nonmagnetic.

4 Do nonmagnetic materials affect the magnetic force?

You may have experimented with making a magnet move on top of a table by moving a second magnet underneath the table. Does the table affect the strength of the magnetic force? In this part of the Investigation, you will find out if magnetic forces get weaker or stronger passing through nonmagnetic materials.

1   From Table 2 above, choose several nonmagnetic materials.

2   Place one magnet on the black rectangle on the ruler below and slide a second magnet closer and closer until the first magnet moves.

3   Record the distance in table 3 when you first see movement.

4   Put each nonmagnetic material between the two magnets and repeat the experiment.

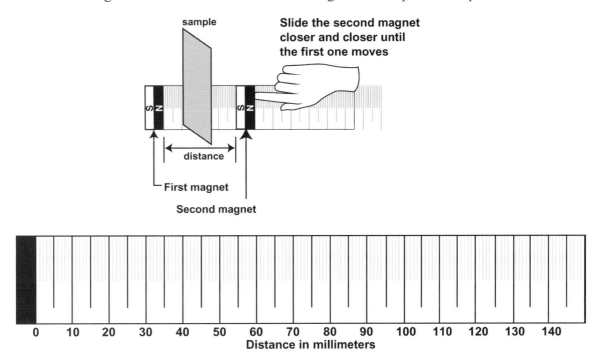

Table 3: Testing nonmagnetic materials

	N-S	S-S	N-N
Distance 1			
Distance 2			
Distance 3			
Average distance			

What did you find out about how magnetism is affected by nonmagnetic materials? Use the words *force* and *distance* in your answer.

Electromagnets

Question: Can electric current create a magnet?

In this Investigation, you will:

1 Build an electromagnet.

2 Measure the electromagnet's strength as the current is varied.

Electromagnets are magnets that are created when there is electric current through a wire. The simplest electromagnet uses a coil of wire, often wrapped around some iron or steel. The iron or steel concentrates the magnetic field created by the current in the coil.

By controlling current, you can easily change the strength of an electromagnet or even turn its magnetism on and off. Electromagnets can also be much stronger than permanent magnets because the electric current can be great. For these reasons, electromagnets are widely used. Stereo speakers, toasters, doorbells, car alternators, and power plant electrical generators are just a few of the many devices that use electromagnets.

Safety Tip: Disconnect your electromagnet when not in use, as the batteries can get hot.

1 **Build an electromagnet**

1 Collect the following materials: three batteries and holders, magnet wire, two nails, a permanent magnet, 10 paper clips, and sandpaper.

2 Wrap one nail tightly with magnetic wire as shown at right. Make sure your wire turns are neat, tight, and evenly spaced or the electromagnet may not work. Use all of the magnet wire except for about 30 cm of wire straight on each end. This is your electromagnet coil.

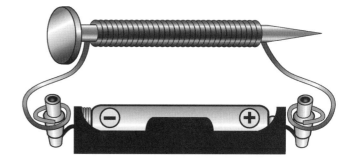

3 Sand the two ends of the wire, as they have a coating on them.

4 Attach the ends of the coil to one battery on the electricity grid. Wrap each end of the electromagnet wire tightly around the posts connected to the battery.

2 **Compare electromagnets and permanent magnets**

a. This coil certainly doesn't look much like the permanent magnets we are more familiar with. Using what you know about magnets from the last Investigation, think of at least two tests to show that your electromagnet acts like the permanent magnets you used in that Investigation. Record your two proposed tests.

b. Perform the two tests. Record your observations.

c. Does the electromagnet act like a permanent magnet? Write down your conclusion, and how you arrived at it.

3   The right hand rule

In an electromagnet, the magnetic poles are located at each end of the coil. Which end is the north pole depends on the direction of the electric current. When your fingers curl in the direction of current, your thumb points toward the magnet's north pole. This method of finding the magnetic poles is called the *right hand rule*.

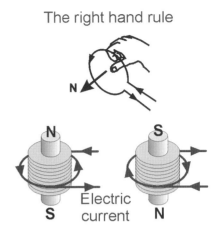

The right hand rule

a. Determine the direction of current through the electromagnet. (The current flows from the positive terminal to the negative terminal.)

b. Use the right hand rule to determine the north and south poles of your electromagnet. Record your answer with a drawing.

4   What happens to the strength of an electromagnet when you increase the current?

1   Measure the current through your electromagnet and test how many paper clips it can pick up.

2   Increase the current through the electromagnet by connecting it to two batteries. Again measure the current and test how many paper clips it can pick up.

3   Repeat step 2 using three batteries.

4   Record all your results in the table below.

Number of batteries	Current (in amps)	Number of paper clips picked up
1		
2		
3		

5   What did you learn?

a. Draw a graph showing how the number of paper clips picked up by the magnet varies as the current is increased. Answer the following questions first: Which variable goes on the *x*-axis? Which variable goes on the *y*-axis?

b. Label your axes and title your graph.

c. What is your conclusion about the relationship between current and strength of the electromagnet?

d. Prepare a poster summarizing the results of this experiment. Include your data table and graph on the poster. Display your electromagnet with your poster.

e. Look at other groups' electromagnets, data tables, and graphs. Did some electromagnets work better than others? Write down anything you notice that might explain differences in performance.

10.3 Electric Motors and Generators

Question: How does an electric motor or generator work?

In this Investigation, you will:

1 Build an electric motor and measure its speed.
2 Design different electric motors and evaluate them for speed and electric power.
3 Build and test several designs of electric generator.

Electric motors are everywhere. You find them in locomotives, washing machines, cars, tools, spacecraft, and anywhere else that we use powered machines. All electric motors use one or both of the two kinds of magnets we just explored, permanent magnets and electromagnets. Permanent magnets are useful because they create the magnetic field without needing any electricity. We will discover that electromagnets are necessary because the north and south poles can be reversed.

1 Getting the rotor to spin

Electric motors spin because of the action of magnetism. Try to get the rotor to spin by manipulating magnets.

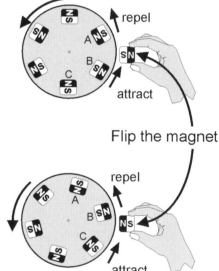

1 Take the motor apart, and put 6 magnets in the rotor so they are evenly spaced and alternate North - South facing outwards.

2 Bring a stack of two or three magnets close and try to repel one of the magnets in the rotor. The rotor should spin a little.

3 As soon as you move one magnet, reverse the magnet in your fingers and try to get attract, then repel the next magnet on the rotor.

4 By sequentially reversing the magnet in your fingers, try to push and pull on the magnets in the rotor to get the motor to spin.

The reversing of the magnet in your fingers is the key to making the rotor spin.

a. When is the right time to reverse the magnet in your fingers? Think about where the magnets in the rotor are.

b. How could you make the rotor spin the other way?

2 Making a 4 pole electric motor

The key to understanding how electric motors work is how electromagnets are used to alternately attract and repel other magnets. If we arrange the electromagnets and permanent magnets just right, the rotor will turn when electricity is connected. The first motor to build is called a 4-pole motor because you are going to use 4 magnets to make 2 north poles and 2 south poles in the rotor.

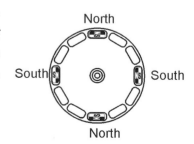

All electric motors use some kind of switch to change the electromagnets from north to south at the right time. The device which makes the electromagnets change form north to south is called the **commutator**. The commutator in the Electric Motor you are building is a plastic disc and it switches the electromagnets using light.

Beam unblocked

Infra-red light beam

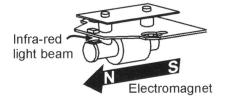

Electromagnet

Beam blocked

Electromagnet

When the light is not blocked (see diagram above) the current flows in a direction to make the north pole at the front of the electromagnet. Blocking the beam causes the current to reverse, making a north pole at the back, and a south pole at the front. There are two green LED's that indicate where the north pole is.

The commutator discs have alternating black and clear sections around the edge that switch the electromagnets by blocking the light beam. Aligning the clear/black edges with the centers of the magnets ensures that the switching happens in the right place.

(1) Find the pink 4-switch commutator disk and adjust it so the switch aligns with a magnet

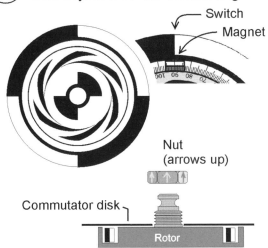

Switch
Magnet

Nut
(arrows up)

Commutator disk

Rotor

(3) Connect batteries

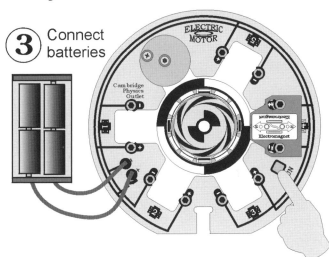

(2) Fasten the commutator disk down with the nut (finger tight)

Slide in an electromagnet and push (and hold) the run button. **(4)**

1   Find the red four-pole commutator disk shown in the picture.

2   Arrange 4 magnets so the north or south poles alternate as shown.

3   Be sure the disk is aligned so the border between clear and black is centered on each of the four magnets. The border is where the electromagnet will switch from north to south and back.

4   Finger tighten the big nut to secure the switch plate once you have it aligned with the magnets.

5   Attach one electromagnet to any position. To make the electrical connections the electromagnet should be pushed forward and the thumb-nuts gently tightened. Don't over-tighten the thumb nuts.

6   Push and hold the RUN button. You usually need to give the motor a push to get it started spinning.

3   Designing and testing different electric motors

Design and test a working electric motor for each of the four program plates shown. Use the design charts to record your design, including the direction (north and south) and position of all magnets. Put an X where you placed the electromagnet. Record only designs that worked. Keep changing things until you get a design that works for each commutator disk.

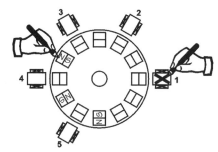

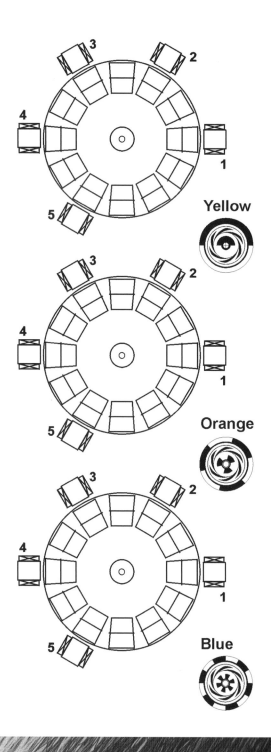

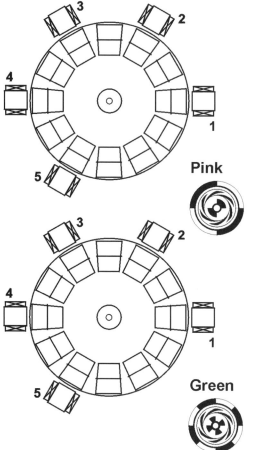

HINTS

The green plate requires you to think differently about how the electromagnet pushes and pulls on magnets in the rotor.

For one of the disks you may want to borrow an extra electromagnet to make it spin

4   Testing for Performance

Engineers usually want to build the best possible machine. Somewhere along the process of design we must define exactly what 'best' means. The word 'best' might mean fastest, least expensive, lightest, strongest, most shock resistant, or most attractive. All practical designs or inventions involve a trade-off between the different definitions of 'best'. It is usually impossible to be best in all categories and the engineer has to choose which categories to be best in depending on what the machine will be used for. One convenient measure for an electric motor is the top speed of the rotor. We can choose the best design as the one that goes fastest.

1   Set up the photogate timer with one photogate attached to the motor as shown. When the photogate is all the way in the slot, the black and clear segments of the disk break the beam as the motor spins.

2   Set the timer to measure FREQUENCY. When measuring frequency, the timer counts the number of times the beam is broken in one second. As the motor speeds up, the light beam gets broken more times per second.

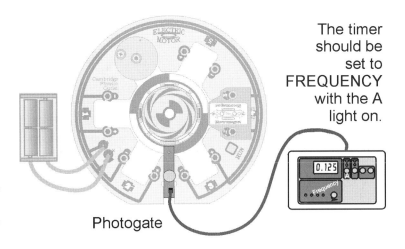

The timer should be set to FREQUENCY with the A light on.

Photogate

$$\text{Rotation speed (rpm)} = \frac{\text{frequency}}{\text{Number of black segments}} \times 60 \, \frac{\text{sec}}{\text{min}}$$

We want to calculate the speed in revolutions per minute (rpm). The formula above shows you how to calculate the speed if you know how many times the light beam gets broken for each turn of the disk.

You can adjust things to make the motor go faster. Adjust your design until you have reached what you think is the highest speed you can get.

a.   Which motor design gave you the highest speed and why do you think it was higher than the others? Your answer should identify the commutator disk and number of magnets you used.

b.   What variables did you adjust that had an effect on the speed? Can you give any explanation for why you think the variables you adjusted made a difference to the speed?

c.   What would happen to your speed comparisons if the batteries were fully charged for the first trial but slowly lost their power later in the experiment?

d.   Can you think of a way to be sure the experimental results were not affected by the draining of the batteries? Write down a procedure that would give you a way to check whether the batteries were still the same all through the experiment.

5   How much electricity does a motor use?

It takes electrical current to make the electromagnet work, and voltage to provide the energy to make the current flow.

1   Build a motor design that you know works well.

2   Check the voltage of the battery pack with the motor off. It should be at least 6 volts.

3   To measure voltage, connect the meter to two (+ and -) thumb-nuts anywhere on the motor. Measure the voltage with the motor on, but stopped. Use your finger to stop the motor from turning. Also measure the voltage with the motor spinning. Record the measurements in the table below.

4   Connect the meter in series with the battery pack so you can measure the current used by the motor. Measure the current with the motor on but stopped, and with the motor on and running.

Table 1: Electrical measurements

	Motor on & stopped		Motor on and running
Voltage (volts)		**Voltage (volts)**	
Current (amps)		**Current (amps)**	

a.   Is there a difference in the voltage with the motor stopped compared to when it is running?

b.   Is there a difference in the current with the motor stopped compared to when it is running?

c.   Power is equal to voltage times current. Calculate the power used by the motor when it is on but stopped, and also when it is on and running.

Table 2: Power calculations

	Motor on & stopped		Motor on and running
Power (watts)		**Power (watts)**	

d.   Does the motor use more power when it is running or when it is stopped but still on? Use your observations to explain why electric motors in machines often burn out if the machine jams and the motor is prevented from turning even though the electricity is still on.

e.   When the motor is running, the energy goes to overcoming friction and adding kinetic energy to the rotor by making it go faster. Where does the energy go when you stop the motor from turning but the electricity is still flowing?

f.   How much power does your motor use compared to a 100 watt light bulb? Your answer should show a calculation of how many motors you could run using the electricity used by the 100 watt bulb.

g.   The horsepower is the average power that could be produced by a working horse. One horsepower is equal to 746 watts. Electric motors are usually rated in horsepower. For example, a table saw might have a 1.5 horsepower electric motor. Calculate how many horsepower your motor makes.

6 Electric generators

Moving current in a wire makes magnetism. That is how electromagnets work. The opposite process also works. Moving a magnet near a coil of wire makes current flow in the wire.

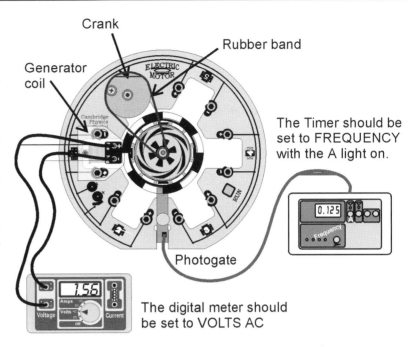

The generator coil does not have the light sensor. The coil of wire is connected directly to the positive and negative terminals.

Connect the meter to the coil terminals and set the meter to measure AC volts.

The Timer should be set to FREQUENCY with the A light on.

The digital meter should be set to VOLTS AC

1   Put two magnets in the rotor on opposite sides of the rotor, with north and south alternating facing out.

2   Put the blue disk on the rotor and fasten it with the nut. It does not matter how you rotate the disk since it is only being used to break the light beam to measure the speed of the rotor.

3   Attach a photogate as you did before and set the timer to measure frequency. The higher the frequency, the faster the rotor is turning.

4   Stretch a rubber band around the crank and the spindle of the motor. You can spin the rotor by turning the crank. The timer will measure the speed and the meter will measure the amount of electricity you generate.

5   With two magnets in the rotor, spin the motor at frequencies of 20, 40, and 80 on the timer. Measure and record the voltage you generate in the table.

6   Repeat the last step with 4 magnets in the rotor, 6 magnets, and 12 magnets. The magnets should always alternate north and south. For each change of magnets, run the same frequencies (20, 40, 80). Record all the data in the table below.

Table 3: Electric generator data (AC volts)

Rotation frequency	Voltage with 2 magnets	Voltage with 4 magnets	Voltage with 6 magnets	Voltage with 12 magnets
20 Hz				
40 Hz				
80 Hz				

Look at your measurements and compare the voltages you got with different numbers of magnets and different speeds.

a.   How does increasing the speed affect the voltage generated? If you double the speed, how much does the voltage change?

b.   How does changing the number of magnets affect the voltage generated? If you double the number of magnets, how much does the voltage change?

11.1 **Harmonic Motion**

Question: How do we describe the back-and-forth motion of a pendulum?

In this Investigation, you will:

1 Measure the amplitude and period of a pendulum.
2 Determine how to change the properties of a pendulum.
3 Design and build a pendulum clock that accurately measures 30 seconds.

Harmonic motion is the term used to describe motion that repeats itself over and over. An oscillator is something that makes harmonic motion. A pendulum is a good example of an oscillator. In this Investigation you will measure and explain the properties of a pendulum. You will need to apply the concepts of cycle, period, and amplitude to accurately describe the harmonic motion of your pendulum.

1 Setting up the pendulum

Attach the pendulum to one of the top holes in the stand.

Attach a photogate so the pendulum bob swings through the light beam. Adjust the position of the string in the slot so the pendulum bob swings through the photogate without hitting the sides. You may also have to adjust the leveling feet at the bottom of the stand.

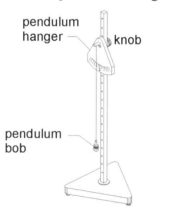

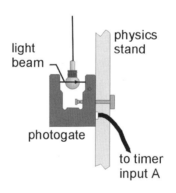

Put the Timer in period mode and attach a single photogate to input A. Use the "A" button and the reset button to make measurements.

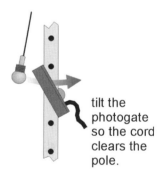

Set the timer to measure period

1 When the A light is on, the display shows the period defined by successive breaks in the light beam.
2 When the A light is off, the timer freezes the last value and stops updating its measurements.
3 The red (O) button resets the timer to zero.

When the pendulum swings through the photogate, the timer will measure the period of time between two light beam breaks. It takes a few swings for the timer to make the measurement.

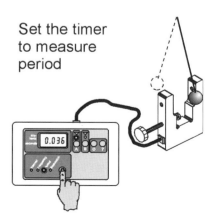

NOTE: The period measured by the timer is the time between the first break and the second break as pictured at right. The pendulum's complete cycle takes twice as long. Therefore its period is twice the measurement from the timer.

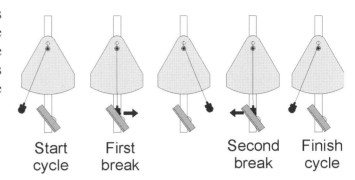

| Start cycle | First break | | Second break | Finish cycle |

2 Testing the three variables

In this experiment, the period of the pendulum is the only dependent variable. There are three independent variables: the mass of the bob, the amplitude of the swing, and the length of the string.

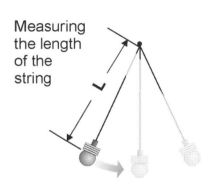

Measuring the length of the string

1   The length of the string can be changed by sliding it through the slot in the peg. Measure the length of the string from the bottom of the string peg to the bottom of the washers.

2   There are washers that you can use to change the mass of the bob.

3   The amplitude can be changed by varying the angle that the pendulum swings.

Design an experiment to determine which of the three variables has the largest effect on the period of the pendulum. Your experiment should provide enough data to show that one of the three variables has much more of an effect that the other two. Be sure to use good technique and provide control of the variables you are not changing.

Period, Amplitude, Mass, and Length Data

Number of washers	Amplitude (degrees)	String length (cm)	Period from timer (seconds)	Period of pendulum (seconds)

3   Analyzing the data

a.   Of the three things you can change (length, mass, and angle), which one has the biggest effect on the pendulum, and why? In your answer you should consider how gravity accelerates objects of different mass.

b.   Split up your data so that you can look at the effect of each of the three variables by making a separate graph showing how each one affects the period. To make comparison easier, make sure all the graphs have the same scale on the y-axis (period). The graphs should be labeled like the example below.

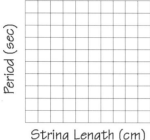
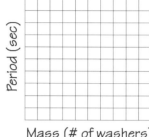

4   Applying what you know

Pendulum clocks were once among the most common ways to keep time. It is still possible to find beautifully made pendulum clocks for sale today. To make a pendulum clock accurate, the period must be set so a certain number of periods equals a convenient measure of time. For example, you could design a clock with a pendulum that has a period of 1 second. The gears in the clock mechanism would then have to turn the second hand 1/60th of a turn per swing of the pendulum.

a.   Using your data, design and construct a pendulum that you can use to accurately measure a time interval of 30 seconds. Test your pendulum clock against the electronic stopwatch.

b.   Mark on your graph the period you chose for your pendulum.

c.   How many cycles did your pendulum complete in 30 seconds?

d.   If mass does not affect the period, why is it important that the pendulum in a clock is heavy?

e.   Calculate the percent error in your prediction of time from your pendulum clock. The percent error is 100 times the difference between your prediction and 30 seconds, divided by 30 seconds.

f.   You notice in a magazine that a watch manufacturer advertises that its quartz watch loses no more than 5 seconds per month. Assume that the watch loses the maximum amount (5 seconds) in 31 days. Calculate the percent error of the quartz watch by comparing 5 seconds to the number of seconds in a month.

5   ## Damping and energy loss

Like all moving systems, oscillators lose energy due to friction. That means any machine that uses an oscillator has to have a way to put energy back in to keep things swinging! Grandfather clocks have heavy weights that slowly fall down and give up their energy to keep the pendulum swinging at a constant amplitude. The weights have to be lifted every few days or the clock runs out of energy and stops.

Set up an experiment to investigate how fast the pendulum loses energy.

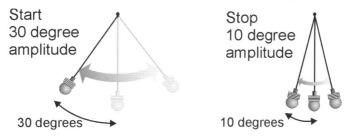

Start
30 degree
amplitude

30 degrees

Stop
10 degree
amplitude

10 degrees

1   To measure the energy-loss record the time it takes the pendulum amplitude to decrease from 30 degrees to 10 degrees.

2   Change the mass four times, keeping string length constant.

3   Change the string length four times, keeping mass constant.

Table 1: Damping Data

Mass (washers)	String length (cm)	Time to decay from 30 degrees to 10 (sec)

a)   Plot two graphs that show how the damping time changes with mass and string length.

b) Suppose you had to design a real pendulum clock that would keep swinging for many days. From the results of your experiment, how would you choose string length and mass? Explain how your choices are based on your observations.

11.2 | Graphs of Harmonic Motion

Question: How do we make graphs of harmonic motion?

In this Investigation, you will:

1   Create graphs showing harmonic motion.
2   Use graphs of harmonic motion to determine period and amplitude.

 ## 1   Simple harmonic motion graph

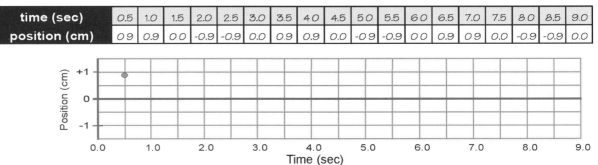 Make a graph from the data table below. Draw a smooth curve that most closely shows the pattern in the data. Answer the questions about the graph.

time (sec)	0.5	1.0	1.5	2.0	2.5	3.0	3.5	4.0	4.5	5.0	5.5	6.0	6.5	7.0	7.5	8.0	8.5	9.0
position (cm)	0.9	0.9	0.0	-0.9	-0.9	0.0	0.9	0.9	0.0	-0.9	-0.9	0.0	0.9	0.9	0.0	-0.9	-0.9	0.0

a.   What is the amplitude of the graph in centimeters?

b.   What is the period of the graph in seconds?

 ## 2   Comparing harmonic motion graphs

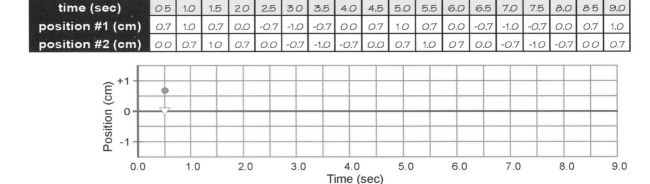 Two different groups of students are doing experiments on giant pendulums with very long periods. Both groups use the same clock to record time. Below are two sets of position vs. time data, one from each group. Graph the data and answer the questions.

time (sec)	0.5	1.0	1.5	2.0	2.5	3.0	3.5	4.0	4.5	5.0	5.5	6.0	6.5	7.0	7.5	8.0	8.5	9.0
position #1 (cm)	0.7	1.0	0.7	0.0	-0.7	-1.0	-0.7	0.0	0.7	1.0	0.7	0.0	-0.7	-1.0	-0.7	0.0	0.7	1.0
position #2 (cm)	0.0	0.7	1.0	0.7	0.0	-0.7	-1.0	-0.7	0.0	0.7	1.0	0.7	0.0	-0.7	-1.0	-0.7	0.0	0.7

a.   Which pendulum was most probably released first? In your answer you must use the word "phase" to explain how you chose which pendulum started first.

b.   How much time was there between the start of the lead pendulum and the start of the other pendulum?

3   **A complex harmonic motion graph**

A clever inventor is trying to build a pendulum that can have two periods at the same time. The pendulum is actually two pendulums, with a very light, short pendulum swinging from a much heavier long pendulum, as shown in the diagram. The position vs. time graph for the combined pendulum was measured. The combined position is the position of the small pendulum while it is swinging from the long pendulum. The graph below shows the motion of the combined pendulum. Answer the three questions from this graph.

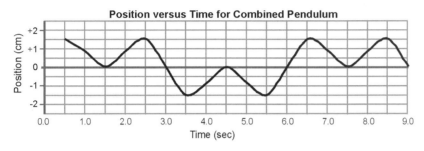

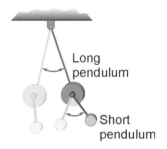

a. What is the amplitude of the combined pendulum in centimeters?

b. What is the period of the combined pendulum in seconds?

c. In one or two sentences, describe the difference between the graphs of the single pendulums and the graph of the combined pendulum.

4   **How you get a complex graph**

The inventor has a theory that the combined motion is the sum of the separate motions of the short and long pendulum. The inventor measured the position vs. time for the short pendulum and the long pendulum separately. To test this theory, add up the positions for the short and long pendulums that were measured separately. For each point in time, write the sum on the line in the table below labeled "Long plus short." Graph the position vs. time for the combined pendulum.

a. Does the graph confirm or disprove the inventor's theory? Explain your answer in a few sentences.

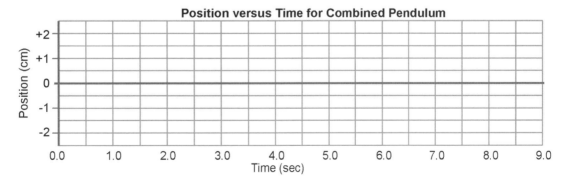

time (sec)	0.5	1.0	1.5	2.0	2.5	3.0	3.5	4.0	4.5	5.0	5.5	6.0	6.5	7.0	7.5	8.0	8.5	9.0
Long Pendulum (cm)	0.5	0.9	1.0	0.9	0.5	0.0	-0.5	-0.9	-1.0	-0.9	-0.5	0.0	0.5	0.9	1.0	0.9	0.5	0.0
Short Pendulum (cm)	1.0	0.0	-1.0	0.0	1.0	0.0	-1.0	0.0	1.0	0.0	-1.0	0.0	1.0	0.0	-1.0	0.0	1.0	0.0
Long plus Short (cm)																		

Position versus Time for Combined Pendulum

11.3   Simple Mechanical Oscillators

Question: What kinds of systems oscillate?

In this Investigation, you will:

1   Create an oscillator and measure its period.

2   Apply the concepts of restoring force and inertia to change the period of your oscillator.

When we disturb a system in equilibrium we often get motion and *sometimes* we get harmonic motion too. A marble on the curved track of the roller coaster is a good example. There is an equilibrium for the marble at the bottom of the valley. If we move the marble partly up the hill and release it, we get harmonic motion. The marble oscillates back and forth around its equilibrium point.

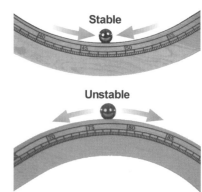

You can also balance a marble on the top of a hill. This equilibrium is different from the one in the valley. If we disturb the marble at the top of the hill it rolls away and does not come back.

The top of a hill is an example of *unstable* equilibrium. In unstable systems there are forces that act to pull the system *away* from equilibrium when disturbed. The bottom of a valley is an example of *stable* equilibrium. In a stable system there are forces always acting to restore the system to equilibrium when it is disturbed. We find harmonic motion in stable systems.

1   Find an example of a stable system and an unstable system

a   Describe your example of a stable system in one or two sentences. What happens when you push it a little away from equilibrium? Write one sentence that describes the motion.

b   Describe your example of an unstable system in one or two sentences. What happens when you push the unstable system a little away from equilibrium? Write one sentence that describes the motion.

2   Making a mechanical oscillator

With mechanical things like a pendulum, harmonic motion comes from the action of forces and inertia. A *restoring force* is any force that always tries to pull a system back to equilibrium. The restoring force (or gravity) always pulls the pendulum toward center no matter which side it is on. Because it has inertia, the pendulum overshoots, passes right through the middle, and keeps going. The restoring force now slows it and accelerates it back toward equilibrium. But, the pendulum overshoots again and goes too far the other direction. The cycle (below) repeats over and over to create harmonic motion.

To make a mechanical oscillator, you need to provide some kind of restoring force connected to a mass that can supply the inertia. A rubber band with a steel bolt tied to the middle makes a perfect oscillator. So does a wok and a tennis ball. See if you can find a creative way to make your own oscillator.

a. Create a system that oscillates. You may use anything you can find, including springs, rubber bands, rulers, balloons, blocks of wood, or anything else that may be safely assembled.

b. Draw a sketch of your system and identify what makes the restoring force.

c. On your sketch, also identify where the mass that creates the inertia is located.

3 Measuring and changing the period of your oscillator

Rubber bands, strings, elastic bands, and curved tracks can all provide restoring forces. Steel marbles, wood blocks, or even the rubber band itself, have mass to supply inertia. To change the period of your oscillator, you need to change the balance between force and inertia.

Period is proportional to the ratio of $\dfrac{\text{Mass (Inertia)}}{\text{Restoring Force}}$

To INCREASE the period ...	To DECREASE the period ...
increase the mass, or	decrease the mass, or
decrease the restoring force	increase the restoring force

a. Estimate or measure the period of your oscillator in seconds. You may use photogates or stopwatches to make your measurements. Describe how you made your measurement and write down some representative periods for your oscillator.

b. Describe and test a way to increase the period of your oscillator. Increasing the period makes the oscillator slow down.

c. Describe and test a way to decrease the period of your oscillator. Decreasing the period makes the oscillator get faster.

4 Applying what you learned

 Trees are oscillators when they sway in the wind, or in an earthquake. A large tree, like an oak, has a very strong trunk and it takes a large force to bend it. A slender tree, like a willow, has a more flexible trunk that can be bent with much less force. Which tree do you think has a longer period of oscillation, a big oak tree or a slender willow tree?

5 Oscillating buildings

If the period is very short, the oscillator cannot move very far in one cycle and the amplitude is small. If the period is long, there is more time for movement and the amplitude can be much larger.

Tall buildings also sway in the wind, and in earthquakes. The same principle applies to buildings as to trees and pendulums. If a building is strong or short it is stiffer. Stiff buildings require more force to bend. A tall thin building, like a tower, bends under less force. Suppose you have a short, stiff building and a tall slender building. In one paragraph, explain which one is likely to sway more in the wind using the comparison of the period and amplitude of each building.

12.1   Waves

Question: How do we make and describe waves?

In this Investigation, you will:

1   Create wave pulses on an elastic cord.
2   Measure the speed at which wave pulses travel.
3   Observe how changing conditions can speed up or slow down a wave.

A wave pulse is a short burst of a wave. The wave pulse is launched and can move and reflect from objects it encounters. Radar uses wave pulses to detect incoming aircraft or speeding cars. An elastic string is a good tool for making wave pulses and learning how they move.

1   Setting up the experiment

You will need about 3 meters of space to make your wave pulses. Two tables or desks spaced apart work well.

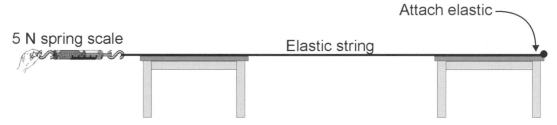

1   Use strong tape (or a knot) to fasten one end of your elastic cord to one table.
2   Take the other end of the elastic cord and make a small knot to attach a spring scale. A scale that can measure 5 newtons of force works well. One person should hold the scale and the other should make the wave pulses.
3   Hold one end of the string against the table top, about 10 centimeters away from the edge, as shown in the diagram. The string should be slightly stretched. One newton of tension works well.
4   Take your other hand and pull the string down about 5-8 centimeters and release it.
5   You will see a wave pulse move down the string away from your hand.

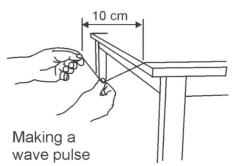

Making a wave pulse

Observe the wave pulse as it moves away from you. Would you describe the pulse as fast or slow?

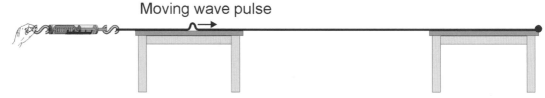

2   ## Measuring the speed of a wave

Because the pulse moves so fast, you will need photogates to measure its speed.

1   Set up two photogates about 1/5 meter apart on the table nearest to where you launch the pulse. The photogates should be upside down and centered on the elastic string as shown in the diagram.

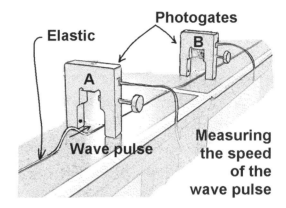

2   Connect the electronic timer in interval mode with both A and B lights on to measure the time interval between photogate A and photogate B.

3   When you snap the pulse it will break the beam first in A then in B. You can calculate the speed of the pulse by dividing the distance from A to B by the time it takes to get from A to B.

4   Not every pulse will give you an accurate reading. The string bounces a lot and each bounce breaks the beam. You only want to record times when you are sure the movement of the pulse is what triggered the photogates at both A and B. For tensions greater than 1/2 newton, the times will should fall between 0.0100 seconds and 0.0200 seconds. Measurements longer than 0.04 seconds are probably due to extra bounces of the string, so they should not be kept.

Make a few trials and calculate the speed of the wave pulse. If you are careful to keep the string stretched the same amount, your timing data should be repeatable to about 0.001 seconds or better.

Table 1: Initial data on the speed of the wave pulse

Trial #	Distance between photogates (m)	Time from A to B (seconds)	Speed of pulse (m/sec)

3   ## Changing the string tension

Try measuring the speed of the wave pulse with the string stretched tighter. Tensions between 1 newton and about 3 newtons will give you good results.

a.   What effect does changing the tension have on the speed of the wave pulses?

b.   From what you know about forces, explain why you think the higher tension makes the waves move faster.

Table 2: String tension data

String tension (N)	Distance between photogates (m)	Time from A to B (seconds)	Speed of pulse (m/sec)

12.2 Waves in Motion

Question: How do waves move and interact with things?

In this Investigation, you will:

1 Create waves in water.
2 Observe how waves can pass through holes and bend around corners.
3 Observe how waves reflect from boundaries.

Waves are oscillations that spread out from where they start. A ball floating on the water is a good example of the difference between a wave and ordinary harmonic motion. If you poke the ball, it moves up and down (A). The oscillating ball creates a wave on the surface of the water that spreads outward, carrying the oscillation to other places (B). A second ball floating farther away also starts oscillating as soon as the wave reaches it (C). The wave started by an earthquake can travel all around the world and reach places far away from where it began.

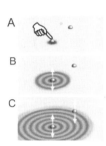

1 Making waves in a ripple tank

Take your flat pan and fill it with about 1/2 centimeter of colored water. The color will help you see the waves.

Find a ruler or other straight object that fits in the tray. If you make a single, gentle back and forth motion with the ruler you can launch a wave that goes across the tray. The ruler makes nearly straight plane waves.

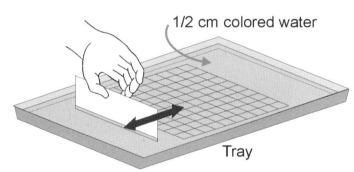

1/2 cm colored water

Tray

a. Draw a sketch that shows the wave front of your plane wave. Also on your sketch, draw an arrow that shows the direction the wave moves.

b. Is the wave front parallel or perpendicular to the direction the wave moves?

c. Would you consider your water wave a transverse wave or a longitudinal wave?

2 Circular waves

Next, take your finger tip and poke the surface of the water. Disturbing the surface in a point makes a circular wave that moves outward from where you touched the water.

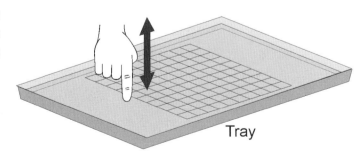

Tray

a. Draw another sketch that shows the circular wave fronts and include at least 4 arrows that show the direction each part of the wave moves.

b. At every point along the wave, are the wave fronts more parallel or perpendicular to the direction the wave moves?

3 Passing through cracks

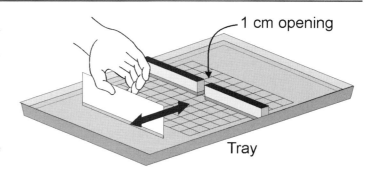

1 cm opening

Tray

1. Take some blocks of wood or other objects and put them in your tray so they block the whole width except for a small opening near the center. The opening should be about a centimeter wide.

2. Make a plane wave that moves toward the center and observe what happens to the part of the wave that goes through the opening.

Diffraction is a process that reshapes waves as they move through and around openings or corners. Because of diffraction, waves spread out after passing through openings or around corners.

a. Sketch the shape of the wave fronts before and after the opening.

b. Does the wave change shape when it passes through the opening? If you see any change, your answer should say what kind of shape the wave changes into.

4 Bouncing off walls

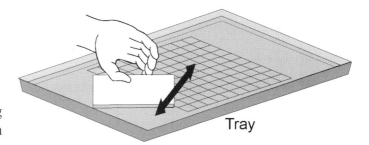

Tray

1. Take the straight wave maker and make a plane wave that moves at an angle toward the edge of the tray.

2. Observe what happens to the wave as it hits the edge.

Reflection is the process of waves bouncing off obstacles, like the side of the tray. When a wave reflects, it changes its direction. The wave may also change its shape.

a. Draw a sketch that shows what happens to the wave front when it hits the side of the tray.

b. Draw an arrow showing the direction of the wave approaching the side.

c. Draw another arrow showing the direction of the wave after it reflects from the side.

d. Do you see any relationship between the incoming and outgoing arrows?

5 Applying your knowledge

a. You can easily hear a person talking through a crack in the door, even though you cannot see them. Do any of your observations provide a clue to why sound can get through tiny cracks?

b. Ocean waves can get many meters high. Big waves on the ocean tend to occur on very windy days. Draw a little sketch and discuss how wind might contribute to making big waves.

12.3 Natural Frequency and Resonance

Question: What is resonance and why is it important?

In this Investigation, you will:

1 Create standing waves on a vibrating string.

2 Learn about resonance.

3 Learn how musical instruments create only the frequencies we want.

You discovered that the pendulum oscillated at only one frequency for each string length. The frequency at which objects vibrate is called the natural frequency. Almost everything has a natural frequency, and most things have more than one. We use natural frequency to control all kinds of waves from microwaves to the musical sounds from a guitar. In this Investigation you will explore the connection between frequency of a wave and its wavelength.

1 Setting up the experiment

Connect the timer to the sound and waves generator as shown in the diagram. The telephone cord connects the timer and wave generator. The black wire goes between the wave generator and the wiggler.

1 Attach the fiddle head to the top of the stand, as high as it goes.

2 Attach the wiggler to the bottom of the stand, as low as it goes.

3 Stretch the elastic string a little (5-10 cm) and attach the free end to the fiddle head. Loosen the knob until you can slide the string between any two of the washers. GENTLY tighten the knob just enough to hold the string.

4 Turn on the timer using the AC adapter.

5 Set the wave generator to WAVES using the button. The wiggler should start to wiggle back and forth, shaking the string.

6 Set the timer to measure FREQUENCY. You should get a reading of about 10 Hz. 10 Hz means the wiggler is oscillating back and forth 10 times per second.

7 Try adjusting the frequency of the wiggler with the frequency control on the wave generator. If you watch the string, you will find that interesting patterns form at certain frequencies.

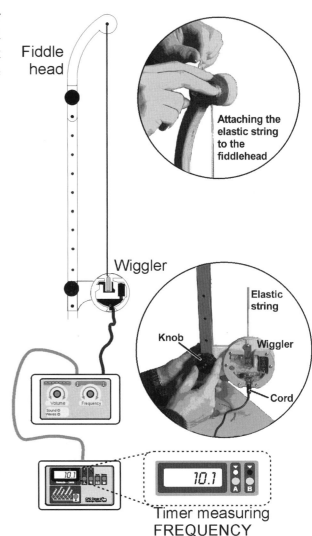

2 Waves and harmonics

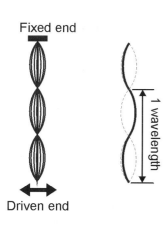

Fixed end

1 wavelength

Driven end

At certain frequencies the vibrating string will form wave patterns like those shown in the picture. Each of the patterns occurs at a *resonance* of the string.

The wavelength of each pattern is the length of one complete wave. One complete wave is two "bumps." Therefore, the wavelength is the length of two bumps. The string is 1 meter long. If you have a pattern of three bumps, the wavelength is 2/3 meter, since three bumps equal 1 meter and a whole wave is two of the three bumps.

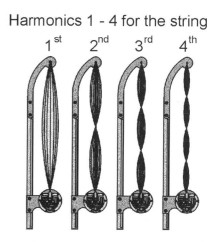

Harmonics 1 - 4 for the string

1st   2nd   3rd   4th

Find the first eight or ten harmonics of the string and record the frequency and wavelength for each one. You should fine-tune the frequency to obtain the largest amplitude before recording the data for each harmonic. Look for harmonics 2-6 before looking for the first one. The first harmonic, also called the *fundamental*, is hard to find exactly. Once you have the frequencies for the others, they will provide a clue for finding the frequency of the first harmonic.

Table 1: Frequency, harmonic and wavelength data

Harmonic #	Frequency (Hz)	Wavelength (m)	Frequency times wavelength (m/sec)
1			
2			
3			
4			
5			
6			
7			
8			
9			
10			

The harmonics greater than 10 are hard to see. You may have to look for patterns of fuzzy-still-fuzzy-still to detect the small movements of the string.

3   Analyzing the data

a. In one or two sentences describe how the frequencies of the different harmonic patterns are related to each other.

b. Why is the word *fundamental* chosen as another name for the first harmonic?

c. In one or two sentences, describe how the product of frequency times wavelength changes compared to the changes in frequency or wavelength separately.

d. If the frequency increases, what happens to the wavelength? Your answer should say if the wavelength changes and by how much it changes compared to the change in frequency.

4   Frequency and energy

Do a few more experiments to measure the amplitude of the wave patterns for each harmonic. The amplitude is 1/2 the width of the wave at the widest point. You should measure at least five different harmonics, including the sixth or higher.

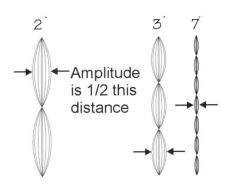

If the amplitude of the wave is larger, the wave has more energy, because it takes more force to stretch the string a greater distance. The wiggler applies electrical energy to vibrate the string. The wiggler supplies about the same amount of energy to each harmonic.

Table 2: Frequency vs. amplitude data

Harmonic #	Frequency (Hz)	Amplitude (cm)

Use your data to answer the questions.

 a. Make a graph showing how the amplitude changes with frequency.

b. Suppose you had a wave maker which allowed you to adjust the input energy so all the waves could have the same amplitude. You then used this wave maker to create two waves with equal amplitude, but one had a higher frequency than the other. If the amplitude is the same, which wave has more energy, the higher frequency wave or the lower frequency wave? In your answer you should use your results to explain why the energy should be the same, higher, or lower.

Equal amplitude but different frequency

Which has the most energy?

5   Force and natural frequency

As you saw with the vibrating string, when you vibrate something at its natural frequency you can get very large amplitude waves. Sometimes you want large amplitude waves, like in a vibrating guitar string. Sometimes you don't want large amplitudes, like in the motion of large buildings.

We often need to change the natural frequency to make it something different. A good example is with buildings. We want the natural frequency for the sway of a building to be different from any frequency likely to occur in an earthquake. Changing the amount of force it takes to move the system is one way to change the natural frequency.

1   Loosen the knob on the fiddle head and attach a spring scale to the end of the elastic string.

2   While the knob is loose, stretch the string until the spring scale indicates the force that you want for the string tension.

3   Gently tighten the knob to hold the string without changing the tension.

4   Adjust the frequency of the wave generator until you have the third harmonic wave. Remember to fine tune the frequency until the amplitude of the wave is as big as it can get.

5   Record the frequency in the data table.

Repeat steps 2-5 for each different string tension.

Table 3: Frequency vs. string tension data

Harmonic #	Tension (N)	Frequency (hz)
3	0.5	
3	1.0	
3	1.5	
3	2.0	
3	2.5	
3	3.0	

6   Applying what you learned

a.   What happens to the natural frequency as you increase the tension of the string? In your answer discuss why this is useful in tuning a musical instrument such as a guitar or piano. You may need to do some research to investigate how guitars and pianos are tuned.

b.   As the tension is increased, making the string stiffer, what happens to the amplitude of the wave? An earthquake is like the wiggler in that it makes the ground shake back and forth with a certain frequency. How do your results relate to making tall buildings sway less in an earthquake? You should consider what happened to the amplitude of the wave when you increased the tension in the string to answer the question.

13.1   Sound

Question: What is sound and how do we hear it?

In this Investigation, you will:

1   Learn about the range of human perception of sound.

2   Learn how to design double-blind experiments.

The ear is a very remarkable sensor. Sound waves that we can hear change the air pressure by one part in a million! In this Investigation, you will earn about the range of frequencies the ear can detect and also how small a difference in frequency we can perceive. Because sound is about perception, and people are different, we will have to use some very interesting techniques to make experiments reliable.

1   How high can you hear?

The accepted range of frequencies the human ear can hear ranges from a low of 20 Hz to a high of 20,000 Hz. Actually, there is tremendous variation within this range, and people's hearing changes greatly with age and exposure to loud noises.

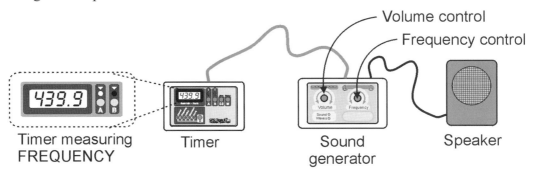

Connect your sound generator to a timer set to measure FREQUENCY. Connect a speaker to the sound generator. When you turn the timer on, you should hear a sound and the timer should measure a frequency near 440 Hz.

There are two knobs for frequency and volume control. Try adjusting the frequency and see how high and low it will go.

See if you and your group can agree on a frequency where you hear the sound as low, medium, high, and very high frequency. Write frequencies of sound that you think sound low, medium, high, and very high. Don't try to be too exact, because the words "low," "medium," and "high" are themselves not well defined. It is difficult to agree exactly on anything that is based completely on individual human perception.

Table 1: How we hear frequencies of sound

Description	Frequency (Hz)
Low	
Medium	
High	
Very high	

2   Testing the upper frequency limit of the ear

To start with a simple experiment, your teacher has a sound generator that can make frequencies up to 20,000 Hz. When the teacher asks, raise your hand if you can hear the sound. Don't raise you hand if you can't hear. Someone will be appointed to count hands and survey the class to see what fraction of students can still hear the sound.

a.   The objective of the test is to see what fraction of people can hear a particular frequency. Once the frequency gets too high, no one will be able to hear it, or at least no humans. Cats, dogs, and other animals can hear much higher frequencies than people. Do you think the method of raising your hands is likely to give a good result? Give at least one reason why you think the method is either good or bad.

Hearing limit survey for 28 adults

b.   Make a bar graph showing how your class responded to frequencies between 10,000 and 20,000 Hz. You should have ten bars, each one for a frequency range of 1,000 Hz. The height of each bar is the number of people who could hear that frequency of sound. If someone could hear the frequency they are counted as a positive response in the graph. This kind of graph is called a *histogram*.

3   Doing a more careful experiment

Another way to do the experiment is with a hidden ballot. The scientist running the experiment will ask if anyone can hear a certain frequency of sound and you check yes or no on a piece of paper. The scientist may play or *not* play the sound. Each frequency will be played five times, and the five repetitions will be all mixed up so there is less chance for error. Every one in the class does one response survey.

Collect the data from the survey sheets class and record it in the chart below.

Survey		
#	Yes	No
1	✓	
2		✓
3		✓
4	✓	
5	✓	
6		✓
7	✓	
8		✓
9	✓	
10	✓	
11		

Key		Played	
#	Frequency	Yes	No
1	12,000	✓	
2	16,000		✓
3	10,000		✓
4	12,000	✓	
5	14,000	✓	
6	14,000		✓
7	18,000	✓	
8	20,000		✓
9	10,000	✓	
10	20,000	✓	
11	16,000		

Table 2: Frequency survey data

# Right	10,000 Hz	12,000 Hz	14,000 Hz	16,000 Hz	18,000 Hz	20,000 Hz
5						
4						
3						
2						
1						

Plot another histogram showing only those people whose choices matched the yes/no on the key for all five times at each frequency. It is hard to fake a response or get it right by chance because you have to choose correctly five times for each frequency. This kind of experiment is called a double-blind test since neither you nor the scientist can see anyone else's response. The results from a double-blind experiment are much more reliable that other forms of surveys. Doctors use the double-blind method to test new medicines.

4   Perceiving differences in frequency

Can you tell the difference between a sound with a frequency of 400 Hz and a sound at 401 Hz? The next experiment on hearing is to test people's ability to distinguish if one sound has higher frequency than another.

In this experiment the scientist will play two frequencies and you mark which one is higher.

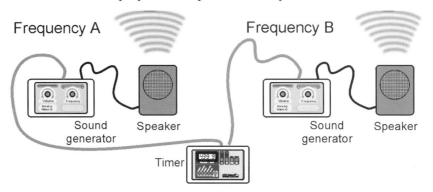

Survey
Which frequency was higher?

#	A	B
1	✓	
2		✓
3		✓
4	✓	
5	✓	
6		✓
7	✓	
8		✓
9	✓	
10		

Key

#	Frequency A	Frequency B
1	400	401
2	404	400
3	390	400
4	1000	1001
5	1050	1000
6	995	1000
7	5005	5000
8	5050	5000
9	4500	5000
10		

To analyze the results you want to know how many people got the right answer for each frequency range. Make a data table like the example below that is large enough to hold all your results.

Table 3: Comparative frequency data

Frequency A (Hz)	Frequency B (Hz)	Frequency difference (Hz)	Percent difference	# of correct responses
1,000	995	5	0.5%	1
1,000	1,050	50	1%	15
1,000	1,001	1	.1%	0

a.   Calculate the percent difference in frequency for each test.

b. There are two ways to look at sensitivity. In one way, we hear *absolute* differences in frequency. If the ear was sensitive to absolute differences, we would hear a 5 Hz difference no matter if the two frequencies were 500 Hz and 505 Hz, or 5,000 Hz and 5,005 Hz.

The second possibility is that we hear relative differences. We might be able to hear a 1 percent difference which would be 5 Hz at 500 Hz. But we could not hear the difference between 5,000 Hz and 5,005 Hz because the percentage difference is only 0.1 percent. To hear a similar difference at 5000 Hz, Frequency B would have to be 5,050 Hz, which is 1 percent higher.

Which model does the data support?

5   Chance and experiments

A very good way to ensure accurate results in a survey test is to make it improbable that anyone could get the correct response purely by chance. A single test is almost never enough to rule out getting a result purely by guessing. Consider that on each test you have a 50 percent chance to guess right. That means one out of every two times you could get the right response just by guessing. This is not very reliable!

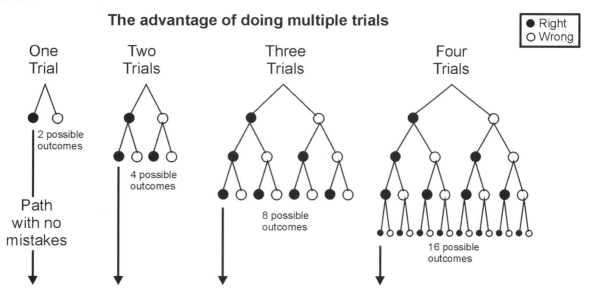

The advantage of doing multiple trials

The diagram shows a decision tree for an experiment with multiple trials. There is only one path with no mistakes. With each additional trial, the total number of possible outcomes increases by 2. With two trials you have one right path out of 4 choices. That means there is only a 1 in 4 chance someone could guess twice correctly. With three trials there is only a 1 in 8 chance of guessing. With four trials the chance of guessing is down to 1 in 16.

a. What is the chance of guessing correctly with five trials?

b. If 100 people did a test with five trials, and everybody guessed, how many people would be likely to make five correct choices in a row?

13.2 Properties of Sound

Question: Does sound behave like other waves?

In this Investigation, you will:

1. Listen to beats and show how they can be explained if sound is a wave.
2. Create interference of sound waves.

Sound is one of the most important of our senses. We use sounds to express the whole range of human emotion. Scientifically, sound is one of the simplest and most common kinds waves. But, what a huge influence it is on our everyday experience! Sound is a rich and beautiful palette from which musicians create works of joy, excitement and drama.

1 Beats, Consonance and Dissonance

Our ears are capable of hearing many thousands of frequencies at a time. Suppose you have two sound waves traveling toward your ear. What reaches the ear is the addition of the two waves.

1. Set up two sound generators close together on the same table.
2. Tune one to 440 Hz and the other to 441 Hz.
3. Stand back and listen to the sound when both are at equal volume.
4. Turn down the 440 Hz sound and listen only to the 441 Hz sound.
5. Turn down the 441 Hz sound and listen to the 440 only.
6. Turn both back up equal again and listen to the combination.
7. Keep one sound generator at 440 Hz and adjust the frequency of the other one between 430 Hz and 450 Hz. Listen to the combinations of sound.

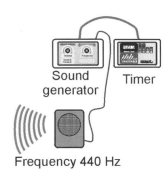

Sound generator   Timer

Frequency 440 Hz

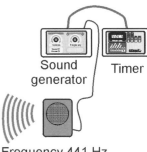

Sound generator   Timer

Frequency 441 Hz

When two waves are close, but not exactly matched in frequency, we hear beats. The beats happen because the waves drift in and out of phase with each other. sometimes they are aligned and the result is twice as loud. A moment later they are exactly opposite and they cancel out leaving periods of quiet. The alternation of loud and soft is what we hear as beats.

Why we hear beats

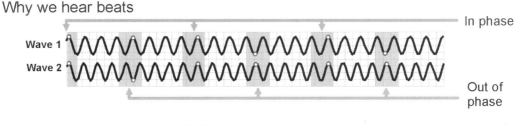

In phase

Out of phase

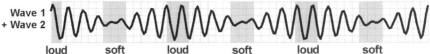

loud   soft   loud   soft   loud   soft

Conduct experiments that can answer the following questions about beats.

a. What makes the beats get faster or slower? In your answer you should describe what you do to the frequencies to make the beats faster or slower.

b. Is the sound of beats pleasant to listen to, or unpleasant? The word *consonant* is used by musicians to describe sounds that fit smoothly together. The opposite of consonant is *dissonant*. Dissonant sounds tend to make people anxious and irritable. Describe the relationship between consonance, dissonance, and beats?

c. How could you use beats to match one frequency to another frequency? This is done every day when musicians in an orchestra tune their instruments.

d. How much different do the two frequencies have to be before you do not hear beats any more?

e. If you have a third sound generator, you can create more unusual beat sounds by having three closely spaced frequencies.

2   Interference

Beats are only one way sound waves interact with each other. Suppose you have two identical sound waves and you are standing where you can hear them both. For certain positions, one sound wave reaches your ear in the opposite phase with the other wave and the sound gets softer, like in beats. Move over a little and the two sound waves add up to get louder. This is called interference and it is easy to demonstrate.

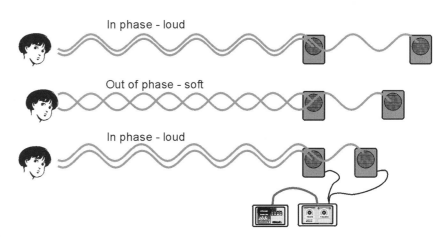

1 Set up one sound generator with two speakers with one speaker about 1/2 meter behind the other.

2 Set the frequency between 400 Hz and 800 Hz.

3 Stand 3 or 4 meters in front of one speaker and have your lab partner slowly move one of the two speakers away. You will hear the sound get loud and soft and loud again when the distance between speakers has changed by one wavelength.

When two speakers are connected to the same sound generator they both make the exact same sound wave. If you move around a room you will hear places of loud and soft whenever your distance from each speaker differs by one wavelength.

a. Try to make an approximate measure of the wavelength of sound by changing the separation of the two speakers, When the sound heard by the observer has gone from loudest, to softest, and back to loudest again the speakers have been moved one wavelength. For this to work you need to keep the observer and both speakers in the same line.

b. Interference can be bad news for concert halls. People do not want their sound to be canceled out after they have paid for the tickets! Why do we not usually hear interference from stereos even though they have two speakers?

Music

Question: What is music and how do we make music?

In this Investigation, you will:

1 Make musical notes by choosing frequencies of sound.
2 Make a simple musical instrument called a straw kazoo.
3 Learn the foundations of musical harmony.

Music is a combination of sound and rhythm that we find pleasant. Some people like music with a heavy beat and strong rhythm. Other people like music where the notes rise and fall in beautiful melodies. Music can be slow or fast, loud or soft, happy or sad, comforting or scary.

1 Making notes

Musical notes are different frequencies of sound. Over thousands of years people have found combinations of frequencies that sound good together. The frequencies are different enough to not make beats but not so different that they cannot make musical melodies that flow.

1 Set up your sound generator and timer.
2 Turn down the volume so you cannot hear the sound but you can still read the frequency from the timer.
3 Each group in the class will be given a different frequency to tune to. Tune your frequency using the timer until you are within 1 Hz of the frequency you were given.

Your teacher will tell you to turn up and down different frequencies so they can be heard together. Don't change the frequency, just adjust the volume up and down when you are asked.

a. Describe the sound of the three frequencies 264 Hz, 330 Hz, and 396 Hz when you hear them together. Which three notes are these? (Look at the diagram below.)

b. Describe the sound of the three frequencies 264 Hz, 315 Hz, and 396 Hz when you hear them together.

c. Contrast the two sounds. Does one sound more happy or sad compared to the other. Does one sound spookier than the other? Which combination reminds you more of spring, which of fall?

d. Describe what adding the 528 Hz frequency does to the blend.

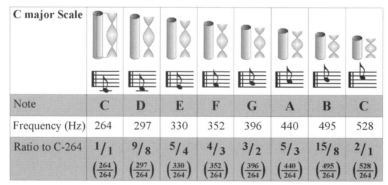

C major Scale								
Note	C	D	E	F	G	A	B	C
Frequency (Hz)	264	297	330	352	396	440	495	528
Ratio to C-264	$\frac{1}{1}$	$\frac{9}{8}$	$\frac{5}{4}$	$\frac{4}{3}$	$\frac{3}{2}$	$\frac{5}{3}$	$\frac{15}{8}$	$\frac{2}{1}$
	$\left(\frac{264}{264}\right)$	$\left(\frac{297}{264}\right)$	$\left(\frac{330}{264}\right)$	$\left(\frac{352}{264}\right)$	$\left(\frac{396}{264}\right)$	$\left(\frac{440}{264}\right)$	$\left(\frac{495}{264}\right)$	$\left(\frac{528}{264}\right)$

2 Controlling frequency and wavelength

Most musical instruments use resonance to make the right frequencies. If the wavelength goes down, the frequency goes up. The way instruments make higher frequencies is to make the wavelengths shorter. The wavelength is controlled by making the vibrating object shorter or longer.

The chart on the last page shows the ratios of frequency to make a musical scale. If the frequency goes up, the wavelength must go down proportionally. That means to double the frequency, the wavelength is reduced by half. To make the frequency 3/2 higher (to get the note E), the wavelength must be 2/3 because $2/3 \times 3/2 = 1$.

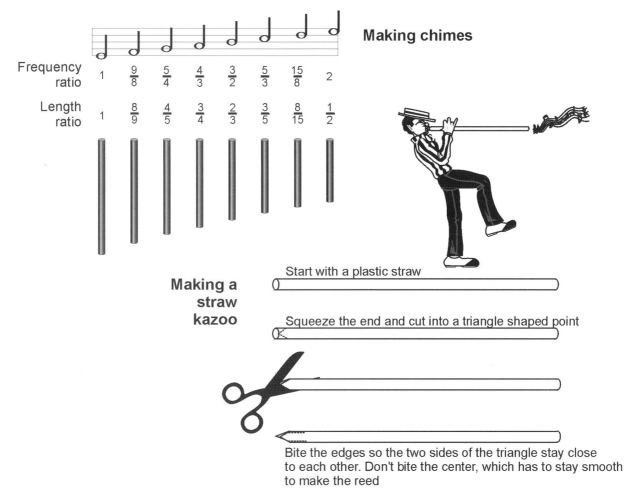

a. Make a straw kazoo and make some sound with it. Take a pair of scissors and cut off the end of the kazoo. What happens to the frequency of the sound it makes?

b. Take the scissors and cut a small hole exactly in the middle of your kazoo. Cover the hole with your finger. Blow through the kazoo and lift your finger to cover and uncover the hole. What happens to the sound? (Hint: What is vibrating in the straw is a length of air.)

c. Identify at least three musical instruments that use vibrating objects of different lengths like the sketch of the chimes above.

Introduction to Light

Question: How can you make light and how can you study it?

In this Investigation, you will:

1 Create light using photo luminescence.

2 Examine colors of light using diffraction grating glasses.

An amazing but very common material is "glow in the dark stuff." Included in the glowing liquid are atoms of the element phosphorus. When light energy hits it, some of the electrons of the phosphorus atom rise to a higher energy state where they either fall right away, or wait for a while before they fall. This is called photoluminescence. The light starts it (photo) and then it gives off more light (luminescence).

The energy that is given off will be in the form of light. It is light energy that begins this process in the first place. Is there a way that we could use this emitted light to cause more electrons to rise?

There are tools that allow us to study light. One of them is called a diffraction grating. When you look through a diffraction grating at a specific light source you will see all the different colors that make up that light. This leads us to the question "What makes different colors?" If electrons falling from a high-energy state to a lower energy state cause light, what do you think would cause different colors of light? That's correct! Electrons falling from different energy levels produce different colors of light. Electrons falling a short distance produce red light and electrons falling a larger distance produce the other colors up to violet. Different atoms have different energy levels and produce different colors.

You can tell a lot about a material based on the colors of light it gives off.

 Safety Tip: Do not try to walk around while the lights are off!

1 **Examine the effects of light on "glow in the dark stuff"**

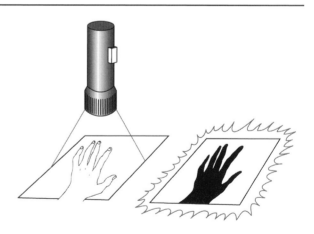

1 While in a dark room, put an object over the "glow in the dark" material.

2 Turn the lights back on, or shine a flashlight onto the "glow in the dark" material. Be careful to keep part of it covered.

3 Turn off the light source, remove the covering and make observations.

4 Record your observations.

5 Expose light energy to "glow in the dark" material without anything covering it.

6 Turn off the light, and then place a piece of white paper over part of the material.

7 Remove the white paper after the glow material starts to dim, and then make observations.

8 Record your observations in your lab notebook.

2 Recording and analyzing your results

a. What happened when the light was not allowed to strike the material? Explain.

b. What happened when light was trapped under the white paper? Explain.

In answering these questions, think in terms of light being energy. Explain what happens to the energy in both of these situations. Record your ideas in your lab notebook.

3 Examining the colors of light given off by a glowing source

1   In this part of the Investigation, you will observe patterns generated by different light sources. Record your observations in the table below.

2   Look through the diffraction grating. You will notice several different rainbows (these rainbows might not be very clear).

3   Turn on the white light source and turn the room lights off. Observe the patterns generated. It is useful to limit your reporting to a single rainbow so, for consistency, refer only to the rainbow to the **left** of the center light.

4   Record the pattern of colors, and spaces between colors, in your table. Use colored pencils, or just label the different color areas.

5   Examine at least three other light sources around the room or building. Use the spectrum to the left of the light and record the patterns in your table. Describe the light source and record your observations in the table below.

Description of light source	Pattern observed using the diffraction grating

4 Analyzing your results

a. Are there some light sources that have identical light patterns? List and describe those here.

5 What did you learn?

a. What must be happening if two different light sources have the same pattern?

b. Could an astronomer use the techniques you used in the Investigation to identify and learn about different stars? Explain your answer.

c. Some materials give off light when they are heated. How could a chemist use the techniques you used in the Investigation to identify and learn about different materials? Explain your answer.

14.2 Color

Question: What happens when you mix different colors of light?

In this Investigation, you will:

1 Experiment with mixing different combinations of colored light.
2 Examine the effects of color filters on white light.
3 Use a spectrometer to determine the exact wavelengths of light.

All the colors of visible light can be created artificially using a combination of three primary colors: red, blue and green. In this Investigation, you will use a white light source and color filters to discover what happens when you mix different colors of light. You will also learn how the filters work.

1 Mixing primary colors of light

1 Construct three colors of light sources by taking three white LEDs (light emitting diodes) and placing color filters over each one.
2 Make a pure white screen with a piece of plain white paper. You may also want to use a white paper cup (or a styrofoam cup).
3 Do the next step with the overhead lights in the classroom off or very dim.
4 Combine different combinations of the light sources by projecting them onto your screen or into the cup as shown in the diagram to the right. You can adjust the distance of your light sources from the screen or cup until you see a definite color of light appear. Record the color you see for each combination in Table 1.

Table 1: Mixing primary colors of light

LED color combination	Color you see
Red + Green	
Green + Blue	
Blue + Red	
Red + Green + Blue	

2 Analyzing your results

a. By moving the lights closer and further away, and using the edges and center of the light sources, you can get many different colors. How can you get the same effect without moving the lights?

b. A projection television must have its three light sources set at the same distances from the screen. Since distance can't change, what does change about these light sources in order to achieve all the different colors?

3 Examining white light as it passes through a filter

A red laser can produce a single pure color of red, but a laser is a very special type of light. Making holograms requires a very pure source of light and, as a result, lasers are used to make holograms. You have three different sources of colored light; but just how "pure" are these colors, and what does the colored filter do to the white light beneath it? In this part of the Investigation you will see how your colored filters work.

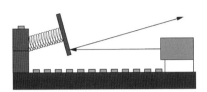

Although pure filters exist, the filters you have tend to "shift" a light source toward a particular color rather than produce a pure light. To study these shifts a precise tool called a **spectrometer** is used. It contains a diffraction grating and a scale for identifying the wavelengths of light that you see. There is a tiny "slit" to allow light in on the right-hand side of one end of the tool. Point the right hand side of this end of the spectrometer at a light source. Look through the diffraction grating (the other end of the spectrometer), and see a rainbow overlaid with a scale. To see this well requires a little practice. The scale in the spectrometer allows you to read the exact wavelengths contained in the light you are viewing. Use the spectrometer and follow the instructions below to see how your colored filters work.

1   Remove the color filter from one of your white LEDs. Examine the white light source with and without the spectrometer. Record the colors you see in Table 2.

2   Replace the color filter on the LED.

3   Examine the three LEDs with the color filters with and without the spectrometer. Record the colors you see in Table 2.

Table 2: Examining LEDs

	Without spectrometer	With spectrometer
White LED		
LED with red filter		
LED with blue filter		
LED with green filter		

4 Drawing conclusions

a.   What does the red filter do to white light?

b.   What does the blue filter do to white light?

c.   What does the green filter do to white light?

d.   How do color filters work?

e.   In a very dark room, place an LED very close to a white screen. Then put the spectrometer very close to the screen so you can examine the reflected light. How is this reflected light different from the light you saw when you viewed the LED directly?

Seeing an Image

Question: What does magnification really mean and how do you plot a reflected image?

In this Investigation, you will:

1 Determine the magnification of a lens.
2 Trace incident and reflected rays from a mirror using a laser.
3 Learn how images are formed in optical systems.

We see **images** that are formed by the eye from light that comes from objects. Because light can be bent by lenses or mirrors, the image we see can be different from the object that produced it. With a magnifying lens, we can make an image seem larger than the object. The magnification is the ratio of real object size to the image size we see through the lens. In this Investigation, you will measure the magnification of a single lens. Another way to change an image is to make it appear to come from somewhere else. The image you see reflected in a mirror, is reversed left-to-right, and in front of where you actually are. In this Investigation, you will learn how to predict where the image in a mirror appears by tracing the incident and reflected rays of light from a laser.

1 **Finding the magnification of a lens**

1 Examine a section of graph paper with your lens. Move the lens closer and farther away until you have the biggest squares you can still see clearly in the lens.

2 Count the number of squares it takes to cross the width of the lens. For example, the picture shows 4 1/2 squares across the lens.

3 Set the lens back on the paper and measure the width of the lens in squares. In the example, the lens is 10 squares wide.

4 The magnification is the image size divided by the object size. The image size is the width of the lens. The object size is the number of magnified squares you see in the lens. For the example, the 4 1/2 squares seen through the lens look as big as 10 squares seen without the lens. The magnification is 10/4.5, or 2.22.

5 Try the experiment again using a ruler to measure the distance between the lens and the paper. Notice that the magnification changes with different distances.

6 Fill in the table below by measuring the magnification of your lens for at least four different distances.

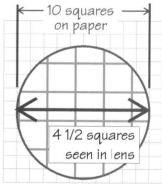

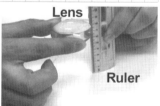

Measuring the distance from the lens to the paper

Table 1: Magnification of a lens

Distance to paper	Squares in lens	Squares on paper	Magnification

2   Reflections in a mirror

1   Fix a sheet of graph paper to the optics table with the magnetic strips.

2   Draw a line on the paper marking where you will place a flat mirror. Place a mirror exactly along your line.

3   Draw a 1 cm long arrow on the graph paper about 3 cm away from your line. The arrow should be parallel to the line.

4   Move your head until you can see the reflection of the arrow in the mirror. The image of the arrow appears to be behind the mirror.

5   Hold your pencil straight up with the point on the tip of your arrow. Use the pencil to set the laser beam so it passes right over the tip of your arrow, and hits the mirror.

6   Trace the laser beam using your pencil as a guide. Trace the beam before it hits the mirror and after it hits the mirror.

7   Move the laser so the beam passes over the tip of your arrow from a different angle, but still hits the mirror. Trace the beam with your pencil like before.

8   The lines you drew represent rays of light before and after they hit the mirror. The **incident ray** shows the light before it hits the mirror. The **reflected ray** shows the path of the light after it bounces off the mirror.

9   Remove the mirror and use a ruler to extend the two reflected rays. They should meet in a point on the other side of the line where the mirror was. This point is where you saw the image of the tip of the arrow. The image is where all rays that leave the same point on an object meet together again.

⬩ **Safety Tip: NEVER look directly into a laser beam. Some lasers can cause permanent damage to your eyes.**

3   Thinking about what you observed

a.   Describe how the magnification changed as you changed the distance from the paper to the lens. Does the magnification get larger or smaller with distance?

b.   Could you adjust the distance between the paper and the lens to get any magnification you wanted, or was there a point where the lens could no longer create a sharp image?

c.   Describe why the image formed by a mirror appears to come from the place where the reflected rays meet. Your answer should use the concept that each point on an object is the source of many rays of light. You might want to include a sketch.

d.   Pick one pair of incident and reflected rays. Draw a straight line perpendicular to the point where the rays hit the mirror. This perpendicular line is called the **normal** in optics. Use a protractor to measure the angle between the incident ray and the normal, and between the reflected ray and the normal. From your angles, what can you say about the relationship between the direction of the incident ray and the direction of the reflected ray?

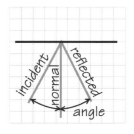

15.2 The Human Eye

Question: How does a lens form an image?

In this Investigation, you will:

1   Trace rays of light through prisms and lenses.

2   Learn how a lens creates an image

3   Find the focal length and magnification of a lens by tracing rays from a laser.

The lens in your eye bends light to form an image on the retina. The lens can change shape so that we can see sharp images close up or far away.

Refraction means 'bending light'. Any clear material can cause refraction. The amount of bending depends on the material and the shape of the surface. In this Investigation, you will explore refraction with prisms and lenses.

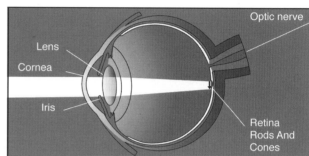

⬥**Safety Tip: Never look directly at the laser beam, or shine the laser beam at another's person's eyes.**

1   Refracting light through a prism

1   Secure a piece of graph paper to your magnetic surface. Put a prism on the center of the paper with the long flat side facing the left of the paper. Trace around the prism with a pencil.

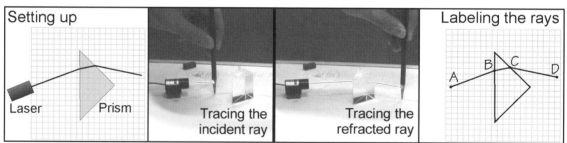

2   Put the laser on the left side of the prism.

3   Shine the laser at the prism and make sure that it comes out the other side of the prism. Use your pencil to find the beam going in and out. The approximate positions in the diagram will work.

4   Use your pencil to trace the path of the laser beam where it goes into and out of the prism.

5   Remove the prism and use a ruler to draw straight lines that follow your rough tracings. Extend the lines until they touch the outline of your prism. Draw a third line to connect the lines through the prism. Label the points at the end of each line with the letters A, B, C, and D as shown in the diagram. Line A-B is the **incident ray**. Line B-C is the path of the laser inside the prism. Line C-D is the **refracted ray**.

6   Try a second time with a different angle for the laser as it approaches the prism. Not all angles will work, for some angles the laser beam will not come out of the right side of the prism at all. Find a few angles for which the beam does go through the prism and trace the incident and refracted rays.

2   Refracting light through a lens

A lens also bends light, like a prism. Because the shape of a lens is curved, rays striking different places along the lens are bent different amounts. The laser allows us to trace how light bends as it passes through a lens.

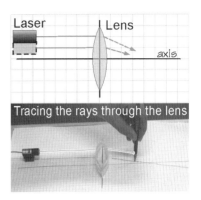

1   Take a large (11 x 17) sheet of graph paper and make a line down the center. Label this the axis. Draw a second line in the middle perpendicular to the first line.

2   Take your 'flat' lens and put in on the intersection of the two lines as shown. Trace around the border of the lens with your pencil.

3   Use the laser to trace four or five rays that approach the lens parallel to the axis. Trace both the incident and the refracted ray.

3   Finding the focus

a.   Rays that approach a lens parallel to the axis meet at a point called the focus. The distance between the midpoint of the lens and the focus is called the focal length. Use a ruler and your experimental ray tracings to determine the focus and the focal length of your lens. Label the focus and focal length on your ray diagram.

4   How lenses form images

When all the rays from a point on an object meet again they form an image. You can use the laser to find where the image is formed from a lens.

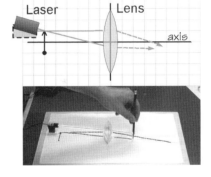

1   Prepare a new sheet of graph paper with lines for the axis and lens, as before. Put the lens at the intersection of the lines.

2   Draw an arrow about 16 centimeters to the left of the lens. The arrow should be about 5 cm tall, centered on the axis. Make a point on one end and a circle on the other end.

3   Use the laser to trace two rays from the tip of the arrow and two rays from the tail of the arrow.

4   The two rays from the tip should meet on the right of the lens somewhere. The two rays form the tail should also meet somewhere on the right.

5   Draw a new arrow with its tip where the rays from the tip meet and its tail where the rays from the tail meet. This shows you the size and position of the image formed by the lens.

5   Characteristics of the image

Compare the image of the arrow to the original arrow.

a.   Is the image larger or smaller? Calculate the magnification by dividing the length of the image by the length of the original arrow

b.   Is the image right side up, or is it inverted?

c.   Is the image closer to the lens than the original arrow, or is it farther away?

15.3 Optical Technology

Question: How are optics used in everyday life?

In this Investigation, you will:

1 Find the critical angle for refracting light through a prism.
2 Learn some of the concepts behind how fiber optics work.

Fiber optics are one of the most important elements of optical technology. A fiber optic is like a wire for light. You can bend a fiber optic and the light will still come through!

Fiber optics work because refraction can turn into reflection if the light rays approach a surface at more than a certain angle. In this Investigation you will find the **critical angle** for a glass prism. Past the critical angle, light is reflected instead of refracted.

1 The critical angle of refraction

1 Take a piece of graph paper and draw a line about 5 centimeters from one edge. Draw an X and an O about the same distance from the line, as shown in the diagram.

2 Fold the paper on the line until it makes an angle greater than 90 degrees, with the X vertical.

3 Place your prism on the graph paper on top of the O. The long face of the prism should be on the paper and the edge aligned with the fold.

4 Look into the prism and move your head up and down to change the angle at which you look in. What happens to the image you see through the prism? Is it an X or an O?

Setting up

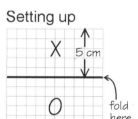

Paper

Prism

Look into the prism at different angles

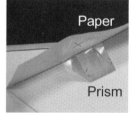

Both refraction and reflection are possible when light hits a boundary between a high index of refraction (like glass) and a lower index of refraction (like air). Whether the light is reflected or refracted depends on the angle. The critical angle is the angle at which the switch from reflection to refraction occurs.

a. Draw a diagram showing the path of the light rays when you see the X.

b. Draw a diagram showing the path of the light rays when you see the O.

c. Is the image in the prism always either reflected or refracted, or can there be both reflection and refraction at the same time?

d. Think about being outside in the bright sun looking into a glass window where it is darker inside the window. Do you see reflection, refraction, or both?

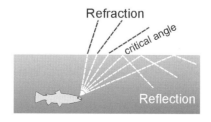

When light is reflected by the boundary between glass and air we call it total internal reflection. The same thing can happen at the boundary between water and air. A fish looking up at the surface of the water from below does not see only the sky! The fish sees reflected rays from the water from part of the surface, and refracted rays from the air from part of the surface.

2   Tracing the critical angle with a laser.

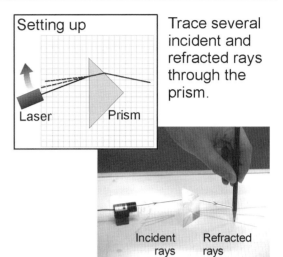

Trace several incident and refracted rays through the prism.

1   Place a prism on the center of the paper. Put the long flat side facing the left of the paper. See diagram at right. Trace the outline of the prism.

2   Put the laser on the left side of the prism. Shine the laser at the prism and make sure that the beam comes out the other side. A good way to do this is to place the laser below the level of the prism and shine it at the upper part of the prism.

3   The beam is entering the prism from air. Using your pencil to trace the beam, observe the angles of incidence and refraction. See diagram to the right.

4   Slowly begin to change the angle of incidence of the initial ray from the laser. Move the laser towards the top of the paper, but keep the beam hitting the prism.

5   You will see the angle of refraction increase until it no longer leaves the prism. This is total internal reflection. The light beam wants to bend more than 90 degrees, which sends it back into the prism. Any decrease in the angle of incidence beyond this point will continue to reflect the laser beam around inside of the prism.

3   Fiber optics

When light is trapped when it enters a fiber optic at less that the critical angle. The light is internally reflected over and over, even if the fiber is bent.

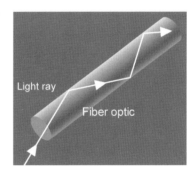

a.   What do you think happens if you try to put light into a fiber optic at the wrong angle?

b.   Do you think it is possible to bend a fiber optic sharp enough that the light leaks out? Explain why you do or do not think this can happen using the concept of critical angle.

4   Observing internal reflection in everyday objects

In this part of the Investigation you will see that any piece of glass or plastic can demonstrate total internal reflection.

1   Find a clear ruler or plastic piece and shine the laser at the edge of it.

2   Observe all the places where the laser beam is exiting the plastic.

3   Observe other materials around the room. Make predictions about whether they will demonstrate total internal reflection. Try out several of these materials.

The next time that you go to a mall look at some of the specialty gift shops that sell interesting lamps and lights. Many of the items you see will contain fiber optic elements to help carry light from one place to another. See how many different varieties of these lights you can find.

16.1

Classifying Matter

In this Investigation, you will:

1   Use a procedure called paper chromatography to separate ink into its components.

Ink is a homogeneous mixture. It consists of a **solute**, which is a collection of colored dye particles, and a **solvent**, which is the liquid that dissolves the solute(s). In this Investigation, you will use a technique called paper chromatography to separate various samples of *water-soluble* ink in order to see the dyes contained in each ink.

1   What is paper chromatography?

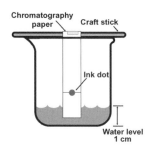

Paper chromatography is used to separate mixtures into their components. A sample of the mixture (ink, in our case) is placed on absorbent paper. The bottom edge of the paper is placed in a liquid. As the liquid travels up the paper, it drags some of the solute particles (the dyes) with it. Different kinds of solute particles have different strengths of attraction to the liquid and to the cellulose fibers in the paper. These characteristics of the solute particles cause them to separate from each other on the paper. Some dyes travel far up the paper and some travel very little.

2   Preparing the samples

1   Cut three strips of chromatography or filter paper. Each strip should be 3 centimeters wide and a little longer than the height of the containers you will be using.

2   On each paper strip, draw a line 1.5 centimeters from one end with a pencil. This end of the paper strip will be called the "ink dot" end. On the other end of the paper, write one of the colors of ink that you will be using (black, blue or green) *and* your initials in pencil.

3   Measure the height of the cup you will be using for the Investigation. On each paper strip, mark this length (the height of the cup) with a pencil. Measure from the "ink dot" end.

4   Place a small dot of black ink (2 or 3 millimeters in diameter) in the center of the line made in step 2. On the second strip, place a blue dot, and on the third, a green dot.

5   Attach each paper strip to a craft stick by rolling the paper strip around the stick as shown in the diagram. Roll the paper until you come to the mark you made in step 3. Use your fingers to press the paper that is wrapped around the stick so that the paper does not unroll. You may want to use a small piece of tape to secure the paper to the craft stick.

3   Setting up the experiment

1   In each of the three cups, pour a small amount of water. The water level should be no higher than 1 centimeter from the bottom of the cup. Use a ruler to measure the water level.

2   Place one paper strip into each cup as shown in the diagram. The paper strip should hang straight down into the water without touching the sides of the cup. Make adjustments to the water level or

the length of the paper strip to prevent the ink dot from being immersed in the water. The Investigation will not work well if the ink dot is underwater!

3   When you have achieved the proper setup, watch the water travel up each strip of paper. Remove the paper from the cup when the water is approximately 1 centimeter from the craft stick.

4   Place the paper strip on a paper towel. With a pencil, carefully mark the water line near the top of the paper strip. Allow the strip to dry.

4   Recording your results

1   In the first column of the table below, the names of the colors of ink are listed. In the second column of the table, list the colors of dye that separated from the ink dot on each of the paper strips.

2   In the third column, record the distance in millimeters from the ink dot to the highest mark made by each color of dye (Dc). Make this measurement for each color on each paper strip.

3   In the fourth column, record the distance in millimeters between the starting line and the water level line on each of your three paper strips. This is the distance traveled by the water (Dw).

4   Calculate the *retention factor* for each of the dye colors. This number shows the ratio of the distance traveled by the dye (Dc) to the distance traveled by the water (Dw). To find the ratio, you need to divide the value for Dc by Dw. Record your results in column five.

Ink color	Dye colors present	Distance traveled by dye color (Dc)	Distance traveled by water (Dw)	Retention factor (Dc ÷ Dw)
black				
blue				
green				

5   Analyzing your data

a.   Which ink contained the greatest number of dye colors? Which colors did it contain?

b.   Did the manufacturer use the same dye color in more than one marker? How do you know?

c.   Compare your chart for the green ink with one other group's chart. Did you see the same separation of colors? Did your dye colors travel the same distance? Did your dye colors have similar retention factors? If you repeated the procedure using a 20 centimeter paper strip, would your retention factors change? Why or why not?

16.2 Measuring Matter

Question: How is matter measured?

In this Investigation, you will:

1 Measure the mass and volume of regular and irregular solids and liquids.

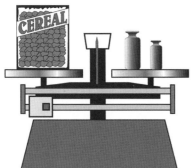

You have learned that matter is defined as anything that has mass and takes up space. In this Investigation, you will practice various techniques for making accurate quantitative measurements of matter. You will learn to use an indirect measurement technique: measuring volume by displacement.

1 Measuring mass

Your materials for this part of the Investigation include a large solid object, a collection of identical small objects, and a container of liquid. Develop a technique for measuring the mass of each object. Record your results in the Table 1.

Table 1: Measuring mass

Object (s)	Description of material	Mass (g)	Description of technique used to find mass
example	*stick of chewing gum*	*3.3 g*	*placed directly on balance*
solid object			
collection			
liquid			

2   ## Measuring volume

You have liquid in a container, a solid object with a regular shape, and an irregular solid. Develop a technique for measuring the volume of each object. Record your results in the Table 2.

Table 2: Measuring volume.

Object	Description of material	Volume in mL or cm^3	Description of technique used to find volume
example	*cereal box*	*4680 cm^3*	*used formula: length $\times$ width $\times$ height*
liquid			
regular solid			
irregular solid			

3   ## Applying your knowledge

a. In step 1, you found the mass of a collection of identical objects. Explain how you could determine the mass of one of those objects without using the electronic balance.

b. Imagine that you had a leaky faucet. How could you find the volume of one drop of water, using only a 100-milliliter graduated cylinder?

c. How could you find the volume of a student? Describe your invented technique.

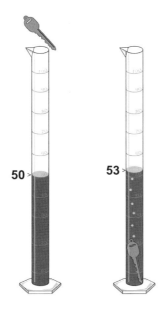

16.3 | States of Matter

Question: How fast can you melt an ice cube?

In this Investigation, you will:

1. Observe the rate at which 15 milliliters of water changes from solid to liquid. Next, you will measure the average kinetic energy of the water molecules as they change from solid to liquid.

2. Analyze the transfer of energy which occurs when a substance undergoes a change of state.

The great ice cube race

In the first part of this Investigation, you and your teammates will race to see who can melt an ice cube in the least amount of time. Your teacher will hand you a sealed plastic bag containing an ice cube. Each cube was formed from 15 milliliters of water, measured at room temperature. It is up to you to find the best technique for melting the ice.

4 Procedure

During steps (1) to (3) hold your zipper-lock bag from the top, without touching the ice cube! If you touch the cube before the race begins, you will be disqualified!

1. Switch the CPO timer to stopwatch mode.
2. Assign one person to start the timer.
3. The first person to completely melt her or his ice cube will stop the timer.
4. Start the timer.
5. As soon as the timing begins, you may pick up your bag of ice. Try to melt the ice cube as fast as possible.
   If you open or break your plastic bag, you will be disqualified!

When the ice cubes are melted, dispose of the water and plastic bags as directed by your teacher.

5 Analyzing your results

a. List at least three techniques used in your group to melt the ice cube.

b. Which technique was most effective? Why?

c. Using what you know about potential and kinetic energy, describe the transfer of energy which occurred as your group's best technique was executed.

6 A closer look at the melting process

You have learned that molecules in a solid vibrate, but do not change position. Molecules in a liquid move and slide around but do not separate one from another. Molecules in a gas move freely, separated from one another. How do we account for this difference?

It has to do with the amount of kinetic energy in the system. As kinetic energy is added to a solid, the molecules begin to vibrate faster. When the molecules have enough kinetic energy to overcome the attractive forces holding them in place, they begin to move and slide around. The solid begins to turn to a liquid.

How can we measure the average kinetic energy of the molecules of our water? The answer is simpler than you might expect. **Temperature** is a measure of the average kinetic energy of the molecules of a mixture or substance. In the second part of this Investigation, you will use a thermometer to gather information about the energy transfer that occurs as ice melts.

7   Procedure

1. In your lab notebook, create a data table with two columns. Label the first column "Elapsed time in minutes" and the second column "Temperature in degrees Celsius."
2. Fill a 150 mL beaker half-full of crushed ice and then add tap water to cover the ice.
3. Reset the stopwatch function of the CPO timer to zero. Place the thermometer in the ice. It should not touch the bottom or sides of the cup. Use the thermometer to gently stir the ice/water slurry.
4. Start the timer.
5. After one minute has passed, record the temperature of the ice. Continue to read and record the temperature every 30 seconds.
6. When you have readings for 3 minutes, one group member should fill a 400 mL beaker half-full of warm water. Another team member should continue to take readings every 30 seconds.
7. Just after taking the 4-minute reading, place the 150 mL beaker into the 400 mL warm water bath. Be sure that none of the warm water gets inside the 150 mL beaker!
8. Continue taking temperature readings until all the ice has melted. Note on your data table where this occurs.
9. Continue taking readings every 30 seconds for 3 more minutes AFTER all the ice has melted.
10. Dispose of the water and cup. Dry the thermometer and return all equipment to your teacher.

8   What did you learn?

a. In your lab notebook, graph the data you collected during this procedure. Label the X-axis "Time in Minutes" and the Y-axis "Temperature in degrees Celsius."
b. Where did the energy that was added to the cup of ice come from?
c. Did the kinetic energy of the water molecules increase at a constant rate throughout the experiment? Use your data as evidence to support your answer.
d. What force had to be overcome in order to change the solid to a liquid?
e. What happened to the energy that was added to the system while the ice was melting?
f. Draw a sketch of the graph you would expect to see as liquid water changes to gas. Write two or three sentences describing the energy changes that occur during this process.

Properties of Solids

Question: How can you find the density of a solid?

In this Investigation, you will:

1   Learn to find the density of various materials.
2   Use the property of density to solve a mystery.

You may be familiar with the trick question "Which is heavier: a pound of feathers or a pound of bricks?" The answer, of course, is that they have the same weight. But why do so many people blurt out "bricks" before they stop to think?

The answer lies in the amount of space occupied by a pound of each material. On the right side of the balance below, sketch a rectangular shape to represent the size of a pound of bricks. Then, on the left side, draw a second rectangle to represent the space taken up by a pound of feathers.

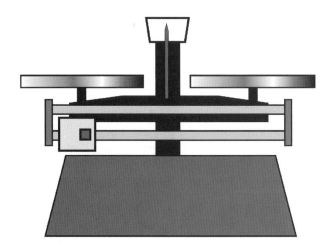

As you can see, a pound of bricks takes up a lot less space than a pound of feathers. The brick-material is squeezed together tightly, while the pound of feathers contains a large amount of empty space.

1   **Setting up**

Each group needs:

*   graph paper and a ruler for each group member
*   balance
*   CPO displacement tank, disposable cup, 250-milliliter beaker, graduated cylinder
*   six small identical objects (provided by your instructor), and approximately 100 pennies

2   Finding the relationship between the mass and volume of a substance

1   Each lab station has a unique set of six objects. Find the mass and volume of each of your objects using experimental techniques. Record your data in Table 1. Note: Although your objects look identical, there may be small differences. Do not obtain your data by multiplying the mass or volume of one object by the number of objects you have.

2   Mass and Volume of Objects

Table 1: Mass and volume data

	one object	two objects	three objects	four objects	five objects
mass in grams (g)					
volume in milliliters (mL)					

3   Plot your data on graph paper. Label the x-axis "volume" and the y-axis "mass." Be sure to use the entire space on your graph paper for making your graph.

3   Analyzing your results

a.   Is there any pattern to the data points on your graph? For example, the points might form a smooth curve, a straight line, a random scattering, or a cluster in a certain region. If you detect a pattern, describe it.

b.   Take your ruler and move it along the points of the graph in order to find the line on the paper that is as close as possible to all of the dots. This line is called the "line of best fit." Draw the line.

Now find the slope of this line. To do so, choose any two points on the line. These will be represented as (X_1, Y_1) and (X_2, Y_2). Use the formula below to calculate the slope of the line:

$(Y_2 - Y_1) \div (X_2 - X_1)$ = slope of the line.

The slope tells how many grams of matter are contained in each milliliter of material you tested. Some substances, like lead, have quite a few grams of matter packed into each milliliter. Other substances, like styrofoam, have less than a single gram of matter packed into each milliliter.

c.   Compare your slope with the result obtained by other groups. Are your slopes similar or different?

d.   The relationship between a substance's mass and volume is called its density. What is the density of the material you tested?

4   Using your knowledge

a.   Your graph includes data for five objects. Now, use your graph to predict the mass of *six* objects.

b.   Now, use the balance to find the mass of six of these objects.

c.   How does your value from your graph compare to the mass obtained using the balance?

d.   Use the mass value that you found in step 4 (b). Find that number on the y-axis of your graph. Now find the point on the line which crosses that y-value. What is the x-value of that point?

e.   What does the x-value found in step 4 (d) predict about the volume of the six objects?

f.   Now, find the volume of six objects experimentally.

g.   How does the x-value from the graph compare with the volume you obtained experimentally?

5 Compare class data

Collect data from each group in the class to fill in Table 2.

Table 2: Class data for density of objects

	Group1	Group 2	Group 3	Group 4	Group 5	Group 6
size of one object (mL)						
type of material						
density						

Using the data above, answer the following questions in your lab notebook:

a. Does density depend on the size of the material? Give evidence to support your answer.

b. Does density depend on the type of material? Give evidence to support your answer.

c. Using what you have observed in this lab, do you suppose that density depends on the shape of the material? Why or why not?

6 Using density to solve a mystery

Many people assume that the United States' one-cent piece, the penny, is made of copper. In fact, the penny has been made from different materials at different times in its history. In 1943, for example, pennies were made of zinc-coated steel, because copper was needed for the war effort. Between 1944 and 1962, pennies were made of bronze, which is a mixture of copper, tin, and zinc. In 1962, their composition was changed to 95 percent copper and 5 percent zinc. Then, in the 1970s, the price of copper increased dramatically, reaching $1.33 per pound in 1980. This meant that the raw material in a penny was worth more than the value of the coin itself. Some members of Congress started to worry that people would start collecting pennies in order to melt them down and sell the copper. As a result, a bill was introduced in 1982 to change the composition of the penny to a less expensive metal with a thin copper coating.

Your job is to use the property of density to determine whether:

a. Congress decided they were overreacting to the situation, and defeated the bill.

Or

b. Congress decided it was worth the trouble to switch to a different material, and passed the bill.

7   Procedure

a. Each lab group has been given a stack of approximately 100 pennies. Sort them into two stacks: pre-1982 and post-1982 pennies. If you find any 1982 pennies, set them aside.

b. Find the mass of your collection of pre-1982 pennies. Use the displacement tank to find the volume of the pre-1982 pennies. Repeat the procedure for your collection of post-1982 pennies. Record your results in Table 3.

Table 3: Penny data

	Pre-1982 pennies	Post-1982 pennies
mass		
volume		
density		

c. Calculate the density of each type of penny. Record your results in the third row of the table.

8   Analyze your results

Using the data you collected, answer the following questions in your lab notebook:

a. Are the pre-1982 and post-1982 pennies made from the same material? Give evidence to support your answer.

b. Did the bill to change the composition of the penny pass or fail?

Density of Fluids

Question: Can you create a stack of liquids?

In this Investigation, you will:

1. Find the density of various liquids, and use this information to create a density column.
2. Use the density column to predict the density of a solid.

Why do you need to shake a bottle of dressing before you pour it on your salad? What does the density of liquids have to do with this? In this Investigation, you will try to stack five liquids in a graduated cylinder in order to build a density column. You will be able to use your density column to predict the density of solid materials.

1 Measuring the density of various liquids

1. You have been given 30 milliliters of five liquids. Use the techniques you have learned for finding the mass and volume of liquids to determine the density of each liquid.

2. Be sure to use no more than 10 milliliters of each liquid in this step of the Investigation. Wash and dry your graduated cylinder between each measurement. Record your results in the table below.

Substance	Mass in grams	Volume in mL	Density in g/mL
molasses			
water			
vegetable oil			
light corn syrup			
glycerin			

2 Deciding how to stack your liquids

A density column is a "stack" of various liquids placed in a tall, thin cylinder. Your task is to create a density column in your 100-milliliter graduated cylinder. First, you will need to decide the order in which the liquids should be placed in the container. Use your density data from the table above to help you decide how to stack the liquids. List the order of your liquids below:

Liquid 5 (top)	
Liquid 4	
Liquid 3	
Liquid 2	
Liquid 1 (bottom)	

3   ## Constructing your density column

a. Use the remaining 20 milliliters of each liquid to create your density column. If desired, add one or two drops of food coloring to the water, corn syrup, and glycerin to make them easier to distinguish.

b. Carefully pour the liquids into the column. Let one liquid settle before adding the next.

4   ## Using your column to compare densities of solid objects

a. A solid object placed in your density column will float if it is less dense than the liquid in which it is immersed, but will sink if it is more dense than the liquid. You have three objects. Predict where each object will stay when placed in the column. Write your predictions in the following table.

Material	Where will it stay?
small steel object	
cork	
rubber stopper	

b. Gently place the objects (one at a time) into the density column.

c. Were your predictions correct? Record your observations of each object's behavior.

5   ## Using the density column to predict the density of the rubber stopper

a. Based on your results from above, predict the density of the rubber stopper. Use the following sentence format: The density of the rubber stopper is between ___ g/mL and ___g/mL.

b. Pour the materials out of the graduated cylinder. All of the liquids may be disposed of in a sink. Clean and dry the graduated cylinder and the three objects.

c. Calculate the actual density of the rubber stopper by obtaining its mass and volume.

d. Does your calculated density match your predicted density based on the density column results? Explain why or why not?

17.3 | **Buoyancy of Fluids**

Question: Can you make a clay boat float?

In this Investigation, you will:

1. Investigate how the shape of an object influences whether it sinks or floats.
2. Explore the relationship between the weight of an object and the weight of the water it displaces.

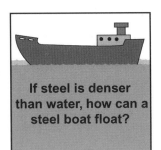

If steel is denser than water, how can a steel boat float?

In the previous Investigation, you learned that a solid material will float if it is less dense than the liquid in which it is immersed, and sink if it is denser than the liquid. You may have noticed, however, that ships are often made of steel, which is obviously denser than water. So how does a steel boat float? In this Investigation, you will experiment with modeling clay to discover how and why boats can be made of materials that are denser than water.

1 ### Finding the density of your stick of clay

1. Before molding your stick of clay, find its density. Use the formula method (length × width × height) to calculate its volume.
2. Predict: Will your stick of clay sink or float? Why?

2 ### Testing your prediction

1. Prepare the displacement tank for use. Place a dry beaker under the spout to catch the overflow.
2. Immerse your stick of clay in water. As soon as the water stops flowing, remove the clay from the water. Set it on a paper towel to dry.
3. Did your stick of clay sink or float?

3 ### Finding the mass and volume of the displaced water

1. Measure the mass of the beaker + displaced water from 2.1 above.
2. Pour the water into a 100-milliliter graduated cylinder. Record the volume.
3. Dry the beaker, then measure its mass.
4. Now, calculate the mass of the displaced water.

4 ### Calculating the weight of the displaced water

1. Mass and weight measure two different properties of matter. Mass refers to how much matter the object contains. Weight measures the gravitational pull between the object and (in our case) Earth. The gravitational force between a 1-kilogram object and Earth is 9.8 newtons, and a 1-gram object's weight on Earth is 0.0098 newtons. You can use this information to calculate the weight of your displaced water from the mass which you found in step 3.4.
   Calculate the weight of the displaced water. Use the formula: grams × (0.0098N/gram) = newtons.

5   ## Calculating the weight of your clay

1   From the mass of your clay (found in step 1), calculate its weight.
Again, use the formula: grams $\times$ (0.0098 N/grams) = newtons.

6   ## Challenge: Can you mold your clay into a shape that floats?

1   You know that steel can be fashioned into a shape that floats. Can you do the same thing with clay?
For this part of the Investigation, you must use ALL of your clay. Mold it into a shape that you
believe will float.

2   When you are ready to test a shape, lower it into a container of water approximately three-quarters
full. If the clay sinks, retrieve it immediately and dry it with a paper towel. Avoid mixing water into
your clay, or it will get very slimy. When your clay is dry, modify your "boat" and try again.

3   When you have successfully molded a boat that floats, take it out of the water and dry it with a
paper towel. Then, prepare your displacement tank just as you did in step 2. Carefully place your
boat into the displacement tank. Avoid making waves. When the water stops flowing, move the
beaker away from the displacement tank spout. Retrieve your boat and set it aside to dry.

4   Find the mass of the beaker + displaced water. Subtract the mass of the beaker, which you found in
step 3.3. Record the mass of the displaced water.

5   Calculate the weight of the displaced water from its mass. Use the formula given in step 4.1.

6   Pour the displaced water into a graduated cylinder. Record its volume.

7   When your boat is dry, first measure its mass, then calculate its weight.

7   ## Analyzing your data

Enter your data from this Investigation in the table below:

	weight (N)	volume of displaced water	weight of displaced water
stick of clay	(step 5.1):	(step 3.2):	(step 4.1):
clay boat	(step 6.7):	(step 6.6):	(step 6.5):

a.   Did the weight of the clay change during the Investigation? Give a reason for your answer.

b.   Which displaced more water, the stick of clay or the clay boat?

c.   Which weighed more, the stick of clay or the water it displaced?

d.   Which weighed more, the clay boat or the water it displaced?

8   ## Drawing conclusions

a.   When you changed the shape of your clay, what happened to the amount of water it displaced?

b.   Is there a relationship between the weight of a sunken object and the weight of water it displaces?

c.   Is there a relationship between the weight of a floating object and the weight of water it displaces?

d.   If you had a clay boat that weighed 100 newtons, how many newtons of water would it displace?

17.4 Viscosity of Fluids

Question: How can viscosity be measured?

In this Investigation, you will:

1   Learn to measure the viscosity of fluids.

2   Compare the properties of viscosity and density of fluids.

What is viscosity? As you know, it takes a lot longer to pour ketchup from one container to another than to pour the same amount of water. Ketchup has *more resistance to flow* than water. Viscosity is a measure of a fluid's resistance to flow. We say that ketchup is *more viscous* than water.

1 Measuring viscosity

Scientists measure viscosity in various ways. One method is to lower a paddle into a container of fluid. The paddle is attached to a motor. When the motor is switched on, the paddle turns in the liquid. The viscometer measures how much work the motor has to do to turn the paddle a certain number of times. You will measure viscosity by timing how long it takes for a marble to fall 10 centimeters through a tube filled with liquid.

The paddle and the marble viscometers work on the same principle: In order for the paddle or marble to move, the liquid must flow. As you know, two materials cannot occupy the same space at the same time. Therefore, the liquid is displaced by the paddle or marble. Your viscometer measures the relative speed of this displacement.

2 Setting up your viscometer

1   Attach photogate B to the CPO physics stand so that the bottom of the photogate "eye" is 7 centimeters from the physics stand base.

2   Attach photogate A so that the distance between the two photogate "eyes" is 10 centimeters.

3   Turn the CPO timer to interval mode, so that it will measure the distance between A and B. Make sure the red light on each photogate is lit.

4   Stretch a rubber band horizontally around each photogate. This will help hold the graduated cylinder in place.

5   You will be given 150 milliliters of liquid. Pour the liquid into the graduated cylinder until it reaches 1 centimeter from the top.

6   Remove the plastic base from the graduated cylinder.

7   Slide the graduated cylinder into the U-shaped spaces created by the two photogates. Rotate the cylinder so that the photogates' light beams are not blocked by any marks on the cylinder. Check this by making sure that the red light on each photogate is still lit.

8   Reset the timer to zero, if necessary.

3 Using your viscometer

1   Carefully place a black glass marble on the top of the liquid. Do not drop the marble into the liquid or in any way force the marble to move.

2   Watch to make sure that as the marble starts to pass through each photogate, the red light goes off. The red light should come back on after the marble passes each photogate.

3   If the lights indicate that the marble did not break the light beam, pour the liquid back into its original container. Retrieve the marble and then pour the liquid back into the graduated cylinder. Adjust the position of the graduated cylinder. You must make sure that the light beams pass through the liquid; see "Setting up your viscometer," step 2. Then try the procedure again.

4   The timer tells you the time it took for the marble to travel between the photogates. Record this time in Table 1.

5   Repeat this procedure two more times, with your second and third marbles. Do not retrieve the marbles until you have finished all three time trials. You may need to pour off a bit of liquid each time, so that the graduated cylinder is filled up to the point one centimeter from the top.

6   Find the average velocity from the three trials and record this average in Table 1.

Table 1: Average velocity of marble in liquid.

Type of liquid	Distance traveled	Time required	Average velocity of marble
Trial 1			
Trial 2			
Trial3			
Find the average of your three values for velocity and record it here:			

4 ## Comparing class data

Each lab group found the data for a different substance. Record the data for each substance in Table 2.

Table 2: Class data for average velocity of marble in liquids of different viscosities

Substance	Avg. velocity of marble in substance at 20°C
group 1:	
group 2:	
group 3:	
group 4:	
group 5:	

5 ## Analyzing class data

a.   Rewrite the table above, listing the liquids from **least** viscous to **most** viscous.

b.   Compare this data with the data from the density column (Investigation 17.2). Does there seem to be a relationship between density and viscosity at room temperature? In other words, if liquids have low density, do they also have low viscosity? Explain your answer and provide an example to justify your answer.

Atomic Structure

Question: How was the size of an atom's nucleus determined?

In this Investigation, you will:

1   Use indirect measurement to find the radius of a circle.

2   Compare and contrast your work with Rutherford's classic experiment.

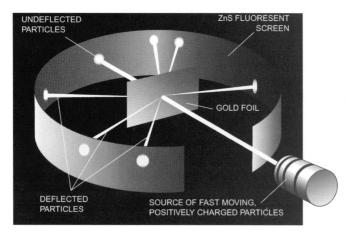

In 1911, British physicist Ernest Rutherford and his colleagues, Hans Geiger and Ernest Marsden, bombarded a thin sheet of gold foil with tiny alpha particles. Most of the alpha particles passed through the foil and hit a screen behind it. But to their surprise, some of the particles bounced back. They must have hit areas of the foil that were more dense! From these results, Rutherford hypothesized that an atom must be made up mostly of empty space, allowing most of the alpha particles to pass through the foil. In the center of the atom, he suggested, there was a tiny core called a nucleus, where most of the atom's mass could be found. In the gold foil experiment, the alpha particles that hit the nucleus of an atom of gold bounced back.

Rutherford and his colleagues set up a ratio of alpha particles that bounced back to total alpha particles. This allowed them to estimate the amount of space taken up by the nucleus in a gold atom. In this Investigation, you will use a similar technique to measure the radius of a circle.

1   ## Using indirect measurement to determine the radius of a circle

1   Place your sheet of carbon paper on the floor, **face up.**

2   Lay the circle-sheet, **circles side down**, over the carbon paper. You should not be able to see the circles during this activity.

3   Tape the circle-sheet to the floor in order to hold it in place.

4   Choose one person to act as the "dropper." The other person will serve as the "catcher." You will switch roles after 25 drops.

5   The "dropper" should hold the marble about 8 inches (the width of a piece of paper) above the paper. You will drop the marble onto the paper. The impact of the marble will cause the carbon paper to make a mark on the circle sheet. Your goal is to cover the paper **evenly** with marble marks. Later you will count the marks to determine the number that fell within the circles compared with the total number of marks.

6   Be sure to catch the marble before it bounces. This ensures that each drop of the marble will make only one mark on the paper.

7   Drop the marble 25 times. If the marble misses the paper, repeat the drop. Switch roles, and repeat the procedure. Continue this process until 100 successful drops have been completed.

2   Recording the data

1   Remove your circle-sheet from the floor. Discard the carbon paper.

2   Count the total number of impact marks on the paper. Do not include those that bleed off the edge of the paper. Record your data in the table below.

3   Count the number of marks that are completely within a circle. Do not include those that touch the edge of the circle. Record your data in the table below.

4   Measure the length and width of the paper in millimeters and calculate its area. Record this information in the table below.

5   We know that the circles are of uniform size and the placement of the marks was random. Therefore, we can set up a proportion:

$$\frac{\text{number of marks in circles}}{\text{number of marks on paper}} = \frac{\text{total area of circles}}{\text{total area on paper}}$$

6   Solve this equation for the total area of circles. Record your result in the table below.

number of marks on paper	number of marks in circles	area of paper in mm^2	total area of circles in mm^2

3   Analyzing your results

a.   Divide the total area of the circles by the number of circles on your paper. This will tell you the area of one circle by **indirect measurement**.

b.   Now, calculate the area of one circle by **direct measurement**. First, use your ruler to find the radius of one circle in millimeters. Use this formula to determine the area of one circle: $Ac = \Pi r^2$ where Ac, the area of a circle, is equal to pi (3.14) times the radius squared.

c.   Compare this value with the radius found by the indirect method. Calculate the percent error of your results: $\frac{(\text{indirect} - \text{direct})}{\text{direct}} \times 100 = \text{percent error}$

4   Drawing conclusions

a.   Write a paragraph to explain how this activity is like the gold foil experiment. Be sure to comment on **each** piece of equipment used. For example, what does the marble represent?

b.   Could Rutherford and his colleagues calculate percent error in the same manner that you did? Why or why not?

c.   What might Rutherford and his colleagues have done to confirm the accuracy of his findings?

d.   Would your percent error have decreased if the marble were dropped 200 times? Or 1000 times?

e.   Name two potential sources of error in your experiment. How could you change the procedure to minimize these errors?

f.   Challenge: Calculate the number of marks that should fall inside the circles on your paper if you dropped the marble 500 times.

Question: What are atoms and how are they put together?

In this Investigation, you will:

1   Learn about the structure of the atom
2   Learn what makes atoms of different elements different from each other.
3   Learn about isotopes and what radioactivity means.

There are three particles that make up all atoms: protons, neutrons, and electrons. In this Investigation, you will learn how atoms of different elements are put together. You will use the atom board to play some interesting games with atomic structure. The marbles will represent the three particles in the atom. Red marbles are protons, blue marbles are neutrons, and yellow marbles are electrons. The position of the marbles on the board shows where the real particles are in the atom. The neutrons and protons are in the nucleus (center) and the electrons are arranged in energy levels around the outside.

 Neutrons *(blue)*

 Protons *(red)*

 Electrons *(yellow)*

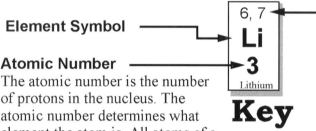

Element Symbol

Atomic Number

The atomic number is the number of protons in the nucleus. The atomic number determines what element the atom is. All atoms of a given element have the same atomic number. For example, all atoms of Lithium (Li) have 3 protons in the nucleus.

6, 7
Li
3
Lithium
Key

Mass Number
The mass number is the total number of particles (protons plus neutrons) in the nucleus. Atoms with the same. number of protons but different mass numbers are called **isotopes.** These numbers are the mass numbers of the stable isotopes. Stable isotopes are not **radioactive.** For example, lithium has two stable isotopes, Li^6 with three protons and three neutrons, and Li^7 with three protons and four neutrons.

1 Setting up

1   Each atom board can have four players.
2   Each player should use one of the four pockets at the corners.
3   Each player should start with the following marbles in their pocket.

> 6 blue marbles (neutrons)
> 5 red marbles (protons)
> 5 yellow marbles (electrons)

4   The remaining marbles stay in the containers and are the 'bank'. Players may need to trade marbles with the bank later in the game.

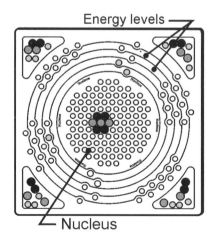

Energy levels

Nucleus

2   The game of atomic challenge

The first player to run out of marbles wins. The object of the game is to play all your marbles by adding them to the board to make real, stable atoms from the periodic table. After each turn you must correctly identify what atom has been made. For example, you might say "Lithium six" if the marbles you added made an atom with 3 protons (red), 3 neutrons (blue) and 3 electrons (yellow).

Each player takes turns adding up to 5 marbles to the atom. The player must add the marbles according to the rules for building atoms:

Example of a good move

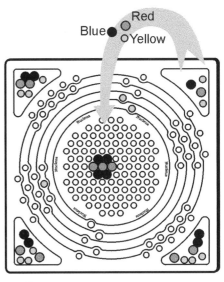

1   The number of protons matches the atomic number (number of red marbles = atomic number)

2   The total number of protons and neutrons equals one of the right mass numbers for that element (number of red + blue = mass number)

3   The number of electrons and protons match (number of red = number of yellow)

4   Protons and neutrons go in the nucleus.

5   Electrons go in the energy levels.

You can add no more than 5 marbles per turn. The 5 can include any mix of colors, such as 2 red, 1 blue, and 2 yellow. You may not always be able to add 5, sometimes you will only be able to add 3 or 4 and still make a real atom. You cannot add more than 5 in one turn.

$$Li^7 + p + n + e = Be^9$$

The periodic table should be carefully consulted by all players to see whether the atom is correct or not. If the atom has been incorrectly built or identified, the offending player must take their marbles back and does not get to try again until the next turn. The next player on the right then takes a turn.

A player can trade marbles with the bank INSTEAD of taking their turn. You can take as many marbles, and of as many colors, as you need, but you must take at least as many total marbles as you put in. For example you can trade 2 yellows for 1 yellow, 1 blue, and 1 red. You put in 2 and took 3, which is OK. You cannot put in 2 and take only 1 back.

3   What did you learn?

a.   What particles are found in the nucleus of an atom? What particles are found outside the nucleus?

b.   Name one element which is always radioactive and which has an atomic number less than 50.

c.   What is the atomic number of sodium (Na)?

d.   How many protons does Na have?

e.   How many different isotopes does magnesium (Mg) have?

f.   How many protons, neutrons, and electrons does Mg^{26} have?

g.   If an isotope of silicon (Si) has 15 neutrons, what is its mass number?

h.   What do you call an atom where the number of electrons is different from the number of protons?

i.   What is the heaviest element with at least one isotope that is NOT radioactive?

j.   What element has atoms with 26 protons in the nucleus?

18.3 The Periodic Table of Elements

Question: What does atomic structure have to do with the periodic table?

In this Investigation, you will:

1   Learn about nuclear reactions.

2   Learn how the different elements of the periodic table were formed.

This Investigation is a game for two to four players called Nuclear Reactions. In order to win, you will need to become quick about figuring out which nuclear reactions will make real atoms. The game is similar to the processes by which the elements of the periodic table were created inside stars. At the center of a star, nuclear reactions combine atoms to make new elements. We believe all the elements of the periodic table heavier than lithium were created inside stars through nuclear reactions. The process gives off a huge amount of energy and that is why the Sun shines. The energy from nuclear reactions in the Sun is what makes life on Earth possible.

Notice that the elements of the periodic table are arranged by **atomic number**, from lowest to highest. The atomic number is equal to the number of protons in the nucleus of an atom. The atomic number also indicates the number of electrons an atom has. Each element has a unique atomic number.

Isotopes are atoms with the same number of protons, but different numbers of neutrons. Isotopes are the same element, but have a different **mass number**. The mass number indicates how many protons and neutrons are in the nucleus of the isotope. The periodic table below shows the mass numbers of the stable isotopes of each element.

1   Starting the game

Each player starts with the same number of each kind of sub-atomic particle in their pocket of the Atomic Structure board. The table below gives the recommended starting number of particles (per player) for different (individual) winning scores. A winning score of 20 makes for about a half hour game.

The deck of Nuclear Reactions cards are shuffled and each player gets five cards which are held and not shown to anyone else.

Players take turns, choosing which (one) card to play each turn and adding or subtracting particles from the atom as instructed on the card. For example, playing an "Add 2 Electrons" card would mean you put two yellow marbles in the atom.

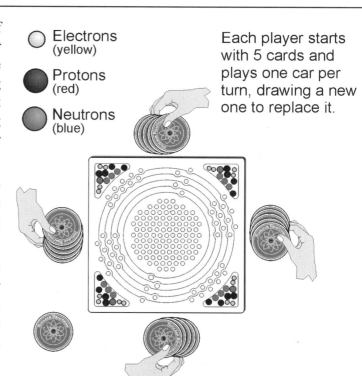

Electrons (yellow)

Protons (red)

Neutrons (blue)

Each player starts with 5 cards and plays one car per turn, drawing a new one to replace it.

Each time you play a card, draw a new card from the deck so you always have a five cards. If necessary the played cards can be re-shuffled and re-used.

Particles added or subtracted from the atom must be played from, or to, your own pocket. You may not play a card for which you do not have the right marbles. For example, a player with only 2 protons left cannot play an "add three protons" card.

The first player to reach 10 points wins.

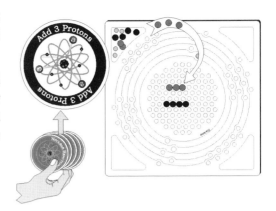

2 Scoring points

1   Points are scored depending on the atom created by your turn. You will need to use the periodic table to determine strategy and points. In particular it is useful to know which cards to play to get to stable isotopes, neutral atoms, or stable and neutral atoms.

The 3 Rules

10, 11	← 2	= ●●●●● Blue
B		+ ○○○○○ Red
Yellow ○○○○○ = 3	→ 5 ← 1	= ○○○○○ Red
Boron		

Rule #1: The number of protons (red marbles) matches the atomic number
Rule #2: The number of protons (red marbles) plus the number of neutrons (blue marbles) equals one of the correct mass numbers for the element of Rule #1.
Rule #3: The number of electrons (yellow marbles) equals the number of protons (red marbles).

You score 1 point if your move creates or leaves a stable nucleus. For example, you score 1 point by adding a proton to a nucleus with 6 protons and 5 neutrons. Adding a proton makes a carbon 12 nucleus, which is stable. The next player can also score a point by adding a neutron, making carbon 13. Points cannot be scored for making a stable nucleus by adding or subtracting electrons, because electrons do not live in the nucleus! To get the nucleus right you need to satisfy rules #1 and #3.

You score 1 point for adding or taking electrons or protons from the atom if your move creates or leaves a neutral atom. A neutral atom has the same number of electrons and protons. Because neutrons have no charge, points cannot be scored for neutrality by adding or subtracting neutrons. Getting the electrons and protons to balance satisfies rule #2.

You score 3 points (the best move) when you add or take particles from the atom and your move creates a perfect, stable and neutral atom. Both adding and subtracting can leave stable, neutral atoms. For example, taking a neutron from a stable, neutral carbon 13 atom leaves a stable neutral carbon 12 atom, scoring 3 points. You get 3 points if your turn makes an atom that meets all 3 rules.

3   ## Miscellaneous rules

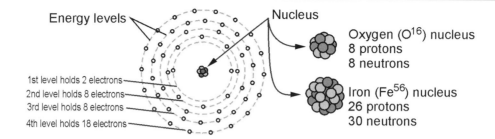

Taking a turn:

When it is your turn you must either

1 Play a card and add or subtract marbles from the atom.

2 Trade in your cards for a new set of five.

Trading in cards

You may trade in all your cards at any time by forfeiting a turn. You have to trade all your cards in at once. Shuffle the deck before taking new cards.

Using the periodic table

All players should be allowed to use the special periodic table of the elements (on the next page) in the course of the game.

The marble bank

You may choose to play two versions of the marble bank.

1 Version 1: Players may take marbles from the bank at any time so they have enough to play the game.

2 Version 2: Players must lose a turn to draw marbles from the bank, and may draw no more than 5 total marbles (of any colors) in one turn.

4   ## Applying what you learned

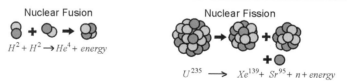

a. There are two basic kinds of nuclear reactions, fission and fusion. Fission splits heavy elements up into lighter elements. Fusion combines lighter elements to make heavier elements. Both can release energy, depending on which elements are involved. What element do you get when you fuse lithium six and boron 11 together? It is stable or radioactive?

b. Write down a nuclear reaction using only two elements that would allow you to build Fluorine 19 starting with Boron 10.

c. Suppose you split a uranium 238 atom. If you have to break it into two pieces, name two elements that could be formed? Be sure that your two elements use up all the neutrons and protons in the uranium. Are either of your two elements stable or is one (or both) radioactive?

Periodic Table of the Elements
with Atomic Numbers and Mass Numbers of Stable Isotopes

Key

Mass Numbers of Stable Isotopes

Atomic Number

6, 7	
Li	Element Symbol
3	Atomic Number
Lithium	Element Name

1,2 **H** 1 Hydrogen																	3,4 **He** 2 Helium
6,7 **Li** 3 Lithium	9 **Be** 4 Beryllium											10,11 **B** 5 Boron	12,13 **C** 6 Carbon	14,15 **N** 7 Nitrogen	16,17,18 **O** 8 Oxygen	19 **F** 9 Fluorine	20,21,22 **Ne** 10 Neon
23 **Na** 11 Sodium	24,25,26 **Mg** 12 Magnesium											27 **Al** 13 Aluminum	28,29,30 **Si** 14 Silicon	31 **P** 15 Phosphorus	32,33,34,36 **S** 16 Sulfur	35,37 **Cl** 17 Chlorine	36,38,40 **Ar** 18 Argon
39,41 **K** 19 Potassium	40,42,43,44,46,48 **Ca** 20 Calcium	45 **Sc** 21 Scandium	46,47,48,49,50 **Ti** 22 Titanium	51 **V** 23 Vanadium	50,52,53,54 **Cr** 24 Chromium	55 **Mn** 25 Manganese	54,56,57,58 **Fe** 26 Iron	59 **Co** 27 Cobalt	58,60,61,62,64 **Ni** 28 Nickel	63,65 **Cu** 29 Copper	64,66,67,68,70 **Zn** 30 Zinc	69,71 **Ga** 31 Gallium	70,72,73,74,76 **Ge** 32 Germanium	75 **As** 33 Arsenic	74,76,77,78,80,82 **Se** 34 Selenium	79,81 **Br** 35 Bromine	78,80,82,83,84,86 **Kr** 36 Krypton
85 **Rb** 37 Rubidium	84,86,87,88 **Sr** 38 Strontium	89 **Y** 39 Yttrium	90,91,92,94,96 **Zr** 40 Zirconium	93 **Nb** 41 Niobium	92,94-100 **Mo** 42 Molybdenum	none **Tc** 43 Technetium	96,104,98-103 **Ru** 44 Ruthenium	104 **Rh** 45 Rhodium	102,108,11,0104-106 **Pd** 46 Palladium	107,109 **Ag** 47 Silver	106,108,114,110-112,116 **Cd** 48 Cadmium	113 **In** 49 Indium	112,114-120,122,124 **Sn** 50 Tin	121 **Sb** 51 Antimony	120,122,123,124-126,130 **Te** 52 Tellurium	127 **I** 53 Iodine	124,126,134,128-132,136 **Xe** 54 Xenon
133 **Cs** 55 Cesium	130,132,134-138 **Ba** 56 Barium	139 **La** 57 Lanthanum	174,176-180 **Hf** 72 Hafnium	180,181 **Ta** 73 Tantalum	180,182,183,184,186 **W** 74 Tungsten	185 **Re** 75 Rhenium	184,192,186-190 **Os** 76 Osmium	191,193 **Ir** 77 Iridium	192,198,194-196 **Pt** 78 Platinum	197 **Au** 79 Gold	196,204,198-202 **Hg** 80 Mercury	203,205 **Tl** 81 Thallium	204,206-208 **Pb** 82 Lead	209 **Bi** 83 Bismuth	none **Po** 84 Polonium	none **At** 85 Astatine	none **Rn** 86 Radon
none **Fr** 87 Francium	none **Ra** 88 Radium	none **Ac** 89 Actinium	none **Rf** 104 Rutherfordium	none **Db** 105 Dubnium	none **Sg** 106 Seaborgium	none **Bh** 107 Bohrium	none **Hs** 108 Hassium	none **Mt** 109 Meitnerium									

136,138,140 **Ce** 58 Cerium	141 **Pr** 59 Praseodymium	142,143,145,146,148,150 **Nd** 60 Neodymium	none **Pm** 61 Promethium	144,152,154,148,149,150 **Sm** 62 Samarium	151,153 **Eu** 63 Europium	152,160,154-158 **Gd** 64 Gadolinium	159 **Tb** 65 Terbium	156,158,160-164 **Dy** 66 Dysprosium	165 **Ho** 67 Holmium	162,164,166,167,168,170 **Er** 68 Erbium	169 **Tm** 69 Thulium	168,176,170-174 **Yb** 70 Ytterbium	175 **Lu** 71 Lutecium
none **Th** 90 Thorium	none **Pa** 91 Protactinium	none **U** 92 Uranium	none **Np** 93 Neptunium	none **Pu** 94 Plutonium	none **Am** 95 Americium	none **Cm** 96 Curium	none **Bk** 97 Berkelium	none **Cf** 98 Californium	none **Es** 99 Einsteinium	none **Fm** 100 Fermium	none **Md** 101 Mendelevium	none **No** 102 Nobelium	none **Lr** 103 Lawrencium

19.1 Bonding and Molecules

Question: Why do atoms form chemical bonds?

In this Investigation, you will:

1   Build models of atoms to gain an understanding of the arrangement of electrons.
2   Identify how atoms form chemical bonds and the role of electrons in bonding.

Most of the matter on Earth is in the form of compounds. Even when a substance exists as a pure element, it tends eventually to combine with other elements. For example, if you leave an iron nail outside in the rain, it will quickly combine with the oxygen in the air to form iron oxide, better known as rust. In this Investigation, you will build models of atoms and discover one of the fundamental ideas in chemistry: how electrons are involved in the formation of chemical bonds.

1   Reviewing atomic structure

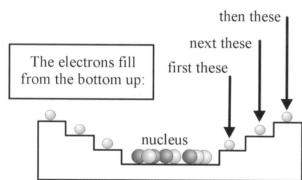

Let's review what you already know about atoms:

• A neutral atom has the same number of electrons and protons.

• The electrons occupy energy levels surrounding the nucleus.

• Since electrons are attracted to the nucleus, they fill the lower energy levels first.

Once a given level is full, electrons start filling the next level.

2   How many electrons are in the outermost level?

Using the atom building game, build each element in the table. For each element, record the number of electrons in the outermost level and the number of unoccupied spaces in the outermost level.

element	atomic number	electrons in outermost level	unoccupied spaces in outermost level
hydrogen			
helium			
lithium			
fluorine			
neon			
sodium			
chlorine			
argon			
potassium			

3   What are valence electrons?

Examine the table you just completed and record the answers to the following questions in your notebook:

a. What do lithium, sodium and potassium have in common?

b. What do fluorine and chlorine have in common?

c. What do neon and argon have in common?

The electrons in the outermost level of an atom are called **valence electrons**. These are the electrons involved in chemical bonds. Lithium, sodium, and potassium each have one valence electron.

4   Modeling a chemical bond

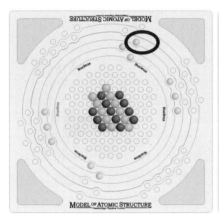 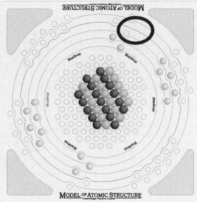

Atoms that have a complete outermost level are stable. If there are empty holes, an atom will either gain, lose, or share electrons with another atom in order to complete its outermost level and become stable. When atoms gain, lose, or share electrons with another atom, they form **chemical bonds**. Using two atom building games, build a sodium atom and a chlorine atom.

Put them next to each other and answer the questions below.

a. In order to complete its outermost level, do you think sodium will tend to lose its only valence electron, or gain seven? Explain your answer.

b. In order to complete its outermost level, do you think chlorine will tend to lose all of its valence electrons or gain one electron? Explain your answer.

c. Why might these two atoms bond together to form a molecule? In your answer, describe what you think might happen when sodium and chlorine form a chemical bond.

5   Determining oxidation numbers

An element's **oxidation number** is equal to the charge an atom has when it **ionizes**, that is, gains or loses electrons.

Use your models of sodium and chlorine to answer the questions below.

a.   Remove the valence electron from sodium. What has happened to the balance of positive and negative charges? What is sodium's oxidation number?

b. Move the electron you took from sodium into the chlorine. What happens to chlorine's charge when it gains the electron from the sodium atom? What is chlorine's oxidation number?

c. When sodium and chlorine form a chemical bond, what is the overall charge of the molecule? Why do you think sodium and chlorine combine in a 1:1 ratio?

19.2 Chemical Formulas

Question: Why do atoms combine in certain ratios?

In this Investigation, you will:

1 Discover the relationship between elements, their placement on the periodic table, and chemical formulas.

2 Build models of compounds using the periodic table tiles and write their chemical formulas.

Chemists have long noticed that groups of elements behave similarly. The periodic table is an arrangement of the elements grouped according to similar behavior. In this Investigation, you will discover how the arrangement of electrons in atoms is related to groups on the periodic table. You will also learn why atoms form chemical bonds with other atoms in certain ratios.

1 Oxidation numbers and ions

An element's **oxidation number** indicates how many electrons are lost or gained when chemical bonding occurs. The oxidation number is equal to the charge an atom has when it **ionizes**, that is, gains or loses electrons to become an **ion**. The partial periodic table below shows the most common oxidation numbers of the elements. The oxidation numbers are written above the group number above each column on the table. Groups 1, 2, and 13 to 18 are called the **main group elements.**

Predicting Oxidation Numbers from the Periodic Table
Partial Table

1+ 1	2+ 2	3	4	5	6	7	8	9	10	11	12	3+ 13	4+ 14	3- 15	2- 16	1- 17	0 18
H 1																	He 2
Li 3	Be 4											B 5	C 6	N 7	O 8	F 9	Ne 10
Na 11	Mg 12	Transition Metals - Variable Oxidation Numbers										Al 13	Si 14	P 15	S 16	Cl 17	Ar 18
K 19	Ca 20	Sc 21	Ti 22	V 23	Cr 24	Mn 25	Fe 26	Co 27	Ni 28	Cu 29	Zn 30	Ga 31	Ge 32	As 33	Se 34	Br 35	Kr 36
Rb 37	Sr 38	Y 39	Zr 40	Nb 41	Mo 42	Tc 43	Ru 44	Rh 45	Pd 46	Ag 47	Cd 48	In 49	Sn 50	Sb 51	Te 52	I 53	Xe 54

a. How are elements grouped according to the number of valence electrons in their outermost levels?

b. Why do elements in group 2 have an oxidation number of 2+?

c. Why do elements in group 17 have an oxidation number of 1-?

d. Why do the oxidation numbers in the first two groups tend to be positive?

2 Predicting chemical formulas

Compounds that are formed from ions are called **ionic compounds**. Predict the chemical formulas for ionic compounds that are made up of the pairs of elements in the table below. Use the following steps:

1 Using the periodic table on the previous page, determine the ion formed by each element.
2 Figure out how many periodic table tiles of each element will be needed to make the compound electrically neutral.
3 Form the compound with your tiles and write the chemical formula for each compound based on the number of tiles of each element

element 1	element 2	ion 1	ion 2	number of tiles of element 1	number of tiles of element 2	chemical formula
hydrogen	fluorine					
magnesium	sulfur					
calcium	bromine					
aluminum	oxygen					
potassium	chlorine					
lithium	argon					

3 Naming ionic compounds

Naming ionic compounds is very simple if you follow these rules:

1 Write the name of the element with a positive oxidation number first.
2 Write the root name of the element with a negative oxidation number second. For example, chlor- is the root name of chlorine. Subtract the -ine ending.
3 Add the ending -ide to the root name. Chlor- becomes chloride.

Using the rules above, write the name of each of the compounds in the table above in your notebook.

Comparing Molecules

Question: What is the meaning of a chemical formula?

In this investigation, you will:

1   Use nuts and bolts to model different combinations of atoms to form compounds.
2   Determine the percent composition of the compounds made out of nuts and bolts.
3   Determine the chemical formula of your compounds based on percent composition of nuts and bolts.

 You have learned that atoms combine in whole-number ratios to form chemical compounds. In fact, the same two elements may form several different compounds by combining in different ratios. Chemical formulas show the ratios in which elements combine to form a compound. In this Investigation, you will use nuts and bolts to illustrate the meaning of chemical formulas.

1   Find the mass of the individual atoms

Your teacher has given you a set of nuts and bolts. Let's assume that the nuts represent atoms of the element **Nu**. Bolts represent atoms of the element **Bo**. Find the mass of one **Nu** atom and the mass of one **Bo** atom and record below:

Mass of **Nu** atom (g): _____   Mass of **Bo** atom (g): _____

2   How many different compounds can you make?

Build five different molecules out of nuts and bolts. You may use any combination you wish. Write the chemical formula for each molecule. Using a balance, measure the mass of each molecule. Next, calculate the percent composition of each element in the molecule by using the formulas provided. Finally, calculate the ratio of **Nu** atoms and the ratio of **Bo** atoms in the molecule using the formulas provided.

chemical formula Nu_xBo_y	mass of I molecule	% **Nu** $\frac{\text{mass of nuts}}{\text{mass of molecule}}$ $\times 100$	% **Bo** $\frac{\text{mass of bolts}}{\text{mass of molecule}}$ $\times 100$	ratio of **Nu** $\frac{\% \text{ of nuts}}{\text{mass of I nut}}$	ratio of **Bo** $\frac{\% \text{ of bolts}}{\text{mass of I bolt}}$

3   Determining the empirical formula of your compounds

As you have learned, elements can combine in many different whole-number ratios to form different compounds. The simplest whole-number ratios by which elements combine are written in a form called the **empirical formula**. The actual number of atoms of each element in the compound is written in a form called the **molecular formula**. For example, H_2O_2 is the molecular formula for hydrogen peroxide. Its empirical formula, or the smallest whole-number ratio is H_1O_1, or simply HO. Determine the empirical formulas for each of your compounds using the following method:

Divide the larger of the two ratios of Nu and Bo by the smaller one. And divide the smaller one by itself to get 1. The result will be the ratio of Nu to Bo. Write the empirical formula for each of your compounds in the table below. If your ratios are not whole numbers, convert them to whole numbers. For example, $Nu_{1.5}Bo_1$ would become Nu_3Bo_2. Finally, write the molecular formula of the compound you made.

ratio of Nu	ratio of Bo	largest ratio smallest ratio Nu or Bo?	smallest ratio smallest ratio Nu or Bo?	Empirical formula Nu_xBo_y	Molecular formula Nu_xBo_y

4   Challenge!

What is the empirical formula and number of molecules of the compound in this box?

Your teacher has handed you a box with a certain number of molecules of Nu_xBo_y in it. Your teacher will share the following information with you: (a) percent that is Nu; (b) percent Bo; (c) mass of 1 molecule of the mystery compound; and (d) mass of empty box. Can you figure out the empirical formula and number of molecules of the mystery compound in the box? For this activity, assume the empirical and molecular formula of your mystery molecule are the same. Show all of your calculations. You may use a balance to find the mass of your box of mystery molecules.

Percent Nu: _____   Percent Bo: _____

Mass of 1 molecule of Nu_xBo_y: _____   Mass of box: _____

Present your findings, and the methods you used, to the class.

20.1 Chemical Changes

Question: What is the evidence that a chemical change has occurred?

In this Investigation, you will:

1   Carry out and observe a series of chemical reactions.

2   Develop a set of rules for determining the occurrence of chemical changes.

Chemical changes are occurring around you all of the time. One way to know that a chemical change has occurred is that the chemical properties of reacting substances are different from the products formed. In this Investigation, you will make a list of the evidence for chemical change by carefully observing a series of chemical reactions.

Safety Tip: Wear goggles and an apron during the entire Investigation

*   Your teacher will provide you with the materials and equipment you need to carry out each chemical reaction.

*   You will complete a total of 6 chemical reactions for this Investigation.

*   Carefully follow the directions provided for each reaction below.

*   Record detailed observations for each reaction in your notebook.

*   Record descriptions of what each substance looks like before and after the chemical change takes place.

*   Properly dispose of all of your reactions after the Investigation.

1   **Reaction #1**

1   Put 5 grams of epsom salts into a baggie.

2   Add 50 milliliters of ammonia solution to the baggie and close it.

3   Feel the baggie with your hands as the reaction proceeds.

4   Record all observations in your notebook.

5   Let the baggie sit until you are finished with the other reactions and record any further observations.

2   **Reaction #2**

1   Place a potato slice into a baggie.

2   Add 50 milliliters of hydrogen peroxide to the baggie and close it.

3   Feel the baggie with your hands as the reaction proceeds.

4   Record all observations in your notebook.

5   Let the baggie sit until you are finished with the other reactions and record any further observations.

3 Reaction #3

1 Put 5 grams of baking soda into a baggie.
2 Add 10 milliliters of red cabbage juice and 50 milliliters of vinegar. Close the baggie.
3 Feel the baggie with your hands as the reaction proceeds.
4 Record all observations in your notebook.
5 Let the baggie sit until you are finished with the other reactions and record any further observations.

4 Reaction #4

1 Put 10 grams of calcium chloride and 5 grams of baking soda into a baggie.
2 Add 50 milliliters of red cabbage juice and close the baggie.
3 Feel the baggie with your hands as the reaction proceeds.
4 Record all observations in your notebook.
5 Let the baggie sit until you are finished with the other reactions and record any further observations.

5 Reaction #5

1 Activate a glow stick as instructed by your teacher.
2 Feel the glowstick as the reaction proceeds.
3 Record all observations in your notebook.

6 Reaction #6

1 Activate a heat pack as instructed by your teacher.
2 Feel the heat pack with your hands.
3 Record all observations in your notebook.

7 Interpreting your observations

1 Look over your observations for each reaction.
2 Consolidate your observations into categories such as: bubble, color change, etc.
3 Identify the evidence of a chemical change for each observation category.
4 Make a table like the one below. An example has been provided.

observation category	evidence of chemical change
bubbles/gas formation	The formation of a gas indicates that a new substance that exists as a gas at room temperature was probably produced.

8 Developing your set of rules

Use the table to develop your set of rules for determining when a chemical change has occurred. Write your rules in your notebook and share them with the class.

20.2 Chemical Equations

Question: How do you balance chemical equations?

In this Investigation, you will:

1   Investigate how atoms are conserved in a chemical reaction.
2   Use the periodic table tiles to learn how to balance equations.

A chemical reaction involves changes in substances that react to form new products. This process involves the breaking of chemical bonds and the formation of new ones. A chemical equation shows the chemical formulas of the substances that react, called **reactants**, and the chemical formulas of the substances that are produced, called **products**. The number and type of atoms in the reactants must be exactly equal to the number and type of atoms in the products. How do you write a chemical equation so that the number and type of atoms on the reactants and products sides are balanced?

1   Writing chemical equations

Magnesium metal reacts with water to produce magnesium hydroxide and hydrogen gas.

The statement above is the word form of a chemical reaction. It tells you the names of the reactants and the products. To write it as a chemical equation, you need to determine the chemical formulas of each of the substances in the reaction:

1   Magnesium metal is an element and exists as an atom. Its chemical formula is Mg.
2   The chemical formula for water is H_2O.
3   Magnesium hydroxide is an ionic compound. To write its chemical formula, you need to find out the charges of each ion it is made out of. The magnesium ion is Mg^{2+}. The hydroxide ion is OH^-. You need 1 Mg^{2+} and 2 OH^- to make a neutral compound so the formula is $Mg(OH)_2$.
4   Pure hydrogen gas always exists as a diatomic molecule so its chemical formula is H_2.

The chemical equation is written as:

magnesium metal	reacts with	water	to produce	magnesium hydroxide	and	hydrogen gas
Mg	**+**	H_2O	⟶	$Mg(OH)_2$	**+**	H_2

2   Trying out the reaction with Periodic Puzzle blocks

Use periodic table tiles to make the reactants above.

Rearrange the reactants to make the products. Is there any problem? What are you missing?

_____

_____

_____

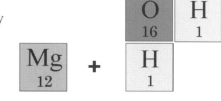

3   Balancing the reaction

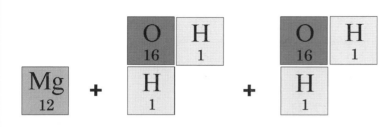

Chemical equations must always balance. This means that you must use all of the atoms you start with and you cannot have any leftover atoms when you are finished. If you need more atoms to make the products, you can only add them in the form of the actual reactants.

You cannot simply add the extra atoms that you need, unless the chemical formula is a single atom - like Mg. Which atoms did you need more of for the reaction you tried? Since you needed more oxygen and hydrogen atoms, you can only add them in the form of another water molecule. Try adding another water molecule to the reactants and rearrange them to form the products again. Did the reaction work this time?

4   Writing balanced chemical equations

To balance the equation for this reaction, you needed to add another water molecule to the reactants side. You ended up with the correct amount of products. Since one magnesium atom reacted with two water molecules to form one magnesium hydroxide molecule and one hydrogen gas, the proper way to write the balanced chemical equation is:

$$Mg + 2H_2O \longrightarrow Mg(OH)_2 + H_2$$

The 2 in front of water is called a coefficient. This number tells you how many water molecules are needed in the reaction. The rest of the reactants and products in the reactants show no coefficients. This is because when the coefficient is 1, there is no need to write it.

5   Try balancing these chemical equations

The following chemical equations have the proper reactants and products. Try to balance each using the following steps:

1   Assemble the reactants out of the appropriate tiles.
2   Rearrange the reactants to form the products.
3   Figure out the number of each reactant and product required to make the equation balance and write the numbers (the coefficients) in the boxes.

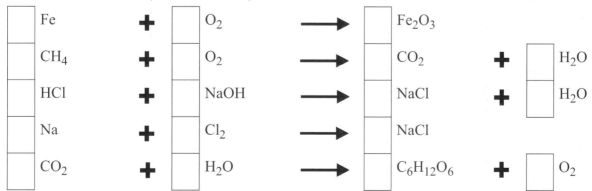

Conservation of Mass

Question: How can you prove that mass is conserved in a reaction?

In this Investigation, you will:

1   Design an experiment to prove that mass is conserved in a reaction.
2   Collect and analyze data.
3   Present the results of your experiment to the class.

 Two hundred years ago, Antoine Laurent Lavoisier, a French chemist, established the **law of conservation of mass** based on his experiments. Lavoisier was the first to recognize that the total mass of the products of a reaction is always equal to the total mass of the reactants. How can you prove his statement to be true? In this Investigation, you will design your own experiment to prove that mass is conserved in a reaction.

1   Testing the reaction

The reaction you will use to prove conservation of mass is one you have probably used before. Have you ever taken an effervescent tablet for indigestion? Before swallowing the tablet, you drop it into a glass of water and allow a reaction to occur before you take the medicine.

Safety Tip: Wear goggles and an apron during the Investigation.

•   Obtain an effervescent tablet and a beaker of water from your teacher. Do not swallow it!
•   Follow the procedures below and record your data as you go.

Step	Data and observations
a. Mass of effervescent tablet. Use a balance to find the tablet's mass. Record it here.	
b. Mass of beaker and water. Find the mass of the beaker and water. Record it here.	
c. Mass before the reaction. Add the two masses and record the result.	
d. Observations. Drop the tablet into the beaker of water. Record your observations.	
e. Mass after the reaction. Let the reaction finish, then tap the beaker gently to release as many bubbles as you can. Find and record the mass of the beaker again.	
f. Mass difference. Subtract e. from c. Record the result.	

2   Was there a difference in mass?

Does this experiment agree with the law of conservation of mass? Explain why or why not based on your results.

Write your answers in your notebook.

3   Proving that mass is conserved in a reaction

According to the law of conservation of mass, the mass of the products of the reaction should be exactly equal to the mass of the reactants. Can you design an experiment to prove this is true for the reaction you just observed?

Examine the materials your teacher has given you. These include:

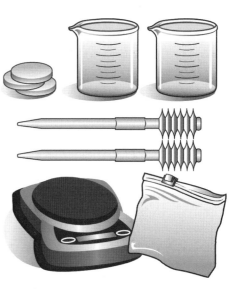

- **effervescent tablet**
- **2 beakers**
- **beaker of water**
- **2 plastic pipettes**
- **2 baggies with zippers**
- **electronic balance or mass scale**

1   Working with your lab partner, devise an experiment that will prove that mass is conserved in the reaction of the tablet and water. You may request additional materials if your teacher has them available.

2   List the materials you will need and their use in the experiment.

3   List the steps you will follow in the experiment.

4   Before you try out your experiment, request approval from your teacher.

5   If your experiment does not work, adjust your procedures and/or materials and try it again.

6   Record your procedures, data and results in your notebook.

4   Presenting your results to the class

Prepare a brief presentation for the class about your experiment. Use the following format for your presentation:

a. Purpose	What questions were you trying to answer?
b. Materials	What materials and equipment did you choose and why?
c. Procedures	What were the steps you followed? You may demonstrate your procedures if time and materials allow.
d. Data	What was the data you collected?
e. Conclusions	What does your data prove? If your experiment did not yield satisfactory results, what would you change in your procedures or materials and why?

20.4 | Using Equations

Question: How can you predict the amount of product in a reaction?

In this Investigation, you will:

1 Follow careful procedures and take accurate measurements of mass.
2 Develop a rule for predicting the mass of product given the mass of the limiting reactant.

 Manufacturers of chemical products need to be able to predict how much product will be made given a certain amount of reactants. In order to harvest the greatest amount of product, they need to make sure that at least one of the reactants is completely used up. To do this, they limit the amount of one of the reactants (usually the more expensive one) and add the other reactant in excess. The reactant that is used up is called the limiting reactant. If manufacturers know the mass of the limiting reactant, they can predict the mass of the products. In this Investigation, you will discover the mathematical relationship that allows them to make this prediction.

1 Writing the balanced equation for the reaction

In this experiment, you will react sodium hydrogen carbonate (baking soda) with acetic acid (vinegar) to produce carbon dioxide gas, water and sodium carbonate. The equation for this reaction is written below. Balance the equation by writing coefficients in front of the reactants and products:

___$NaHCO_3$ + ___$HC_2H_3O_2$ $\longrightarrow$ ___CO_2 + ___H_2O + ___$NaC_2H_3O_2$

2 What does the balanced equation tell you?

Use your balanced equation to complete the table below:

	reactants				products		
$NaHCO_3$	+	$HC_2H_3O_2$	yields	CO_2	+	H_2O	+	$NaC_2H_3O_2$
coefficient	+	coefficient	yields	coefficient	+	coefficient	+	coefficient
formula mass	+	formula mass	yields	formula mass	+	formula mass	+	formula mass

3   ## Doing the experiment and recording the data

For this experiment, you will need to label two beakers, "A" and "B." You will fill beaker B completely with $HC_2H_3O_2$ (vinegar). In the experiment, you will determine the mass of the limiting reactant, $NaHCO_3$ and the mass of one of the products, CO_2. Since CO_2 is a gas, you will obtain its mass through subtraction. It is important to add the reactants slowly and carefully to obtain good results.

Safety Tip: Wear goggles and an apron during the Investigation.

Follow the procedures below and record in the table your data for all four trials.

data and procedures	trial 1	trial 2	trial 3	trial 4
1 *Mass of beaker A.* Find and record the mass of your empty beaker (beaker A).				
2 *Mass of beaker A + NaHCO₃.* Add about 2.0 grams of $NaHCO_3$ to beaker A. Find and record the mass of beaker A + $NaHCO_3$.				
3 *Mass of NaHCO₃ used.* Subtract no. 1 from no. 2. This is the mass of $NaHCO_3$.				
4 *Mass of beaker B with HC₂H₃O₂ before the reaction.* Find and record the mass of the 250 mL beaker full of $HC_2H_3O_2$ (beaker B).				
5 *Mass of beaker B after HC₂H₃O₂ is used in the reaction.* Slowly add $HC_2H_3O_2$, a little at a time, to beaker A. As you add, swirl beaker A gently to dissipate the bubbles of CO_2. Add $HC_2H_3O_2$ until the bubbling stops. Find and record the mass of beaker B again.				
6 *Mass of HC₂H₃O₂ used.* Subtract no. 5 from no. 4. Record the result.				
7 *Mass of beaker A before the reaction.* Add nos. 1, 3 and 6. This will give you the mass of beaker A before the reaction occurred. Record your answer.				
8 *Mass of beaker A after the reaction.* Let beaker A sit for a few minutes. Tap it gently to release as much of the CO_2 as you can. Find and record the mass of beaker A.				
9 *Mass of CO₂ produced.* Subtract no. 8 from no. 7. This will give you the mass of CO_2 produced through subtraction. Record your answer.				

4   Identifying relationships between reactants and products in a reaction

How is the amount of CO_2 produced in the reaction you just carried out related to the amount of $NaHCO_3$ used? One way to find out is to determine the relationship between three variables: the **coefficients** (from the balanced equation); the **formula mass**; and the **actual mass** (from the data table). Fill in the table and identify a relationship between the variables by trying out different calculations (multiplying, dividing, adding, subtracting). You may need to round decimals to the nearest tenth in order to identify relationships in your answers.

Trial 1	reactant, $NaHCO_3$	product, CO_2	Trial 2	reactant, $NaHCO_3$	product, CO_2
coefficient			coefficient		
formula mass			formula mass		
actual mass			actual mass		
Trial 3	reactant, $NaHCO_3$	product, CO_2	**Trial 4**	reactant, $NaHCO_3$	product, CO_2
coefficient			coefficient		
formula mass			formula mass		
actual mass			actual mass		

5   Writing your rule for predicting the amount of product in a reaction

Now that you have discovered the relationship between number of molecules, formula mass and actual mass, write a mathematical formula that will allow you to predict the amount of product given the amount of the limiting reactant in a reaction. Your formula should have the limiting reactant variables on one side and the product variables on the other side. Use the following variables in your rule:

Limiting reactant	Product
C_r = coefficient in front of the limiting reactant	C_p = coefficient in front of the product
F_r = formula mass of limiting reactant	F_p = formula mass of product
A_r = actual mass of limiting reactant	A_p = actual mass of product

Your rule:

combination of reactant variables		combination of product variables
	=	

6   ## Testing your rule

Does your rule work? Test it by carrying out the same reaction again, using a different amount of $NaHCO_3$. Record your results below.

$NaHCO_3$ used in reaction   _____

Predicted yield of CO_2 _____

Actual yield of CO_2 _____

7   ## Calculating percent yield

The predicted yield of a reaction is rarely exactly equal to the actual yield. Why do you think there might be differences? The predicted amount of product assumes the reaction will occur under perfect conditions. The percent yield is the actual yield divided by the predicted yield.

$$\text{percent yield} = \left(\frac{\text{actual yield}}{\text{predicted yield}} \right) \times 100$$

Calculate the percent yield for the reaction you just completed.

8   ## Analyzing the Investigation

a. Why was it necessary to measure the amount of carbon dioxide produced in the reaction instead of one of the other products?

b. Why do you think it was necessary to round off your calculations to the nearest tenth in order to identify a relationship between the variables?

c. How could your mathematical relationship be useful to a company that uses chemical reactions to manufacture products?

9   ## Challenge!

You use products made with aluminum metal everyday, but do you ever wonder where this metal comes from? To obtain pure aluminum, aluminum ore is treated with large amounts of heat to produce pure aluminum metal. Oxygen gas is another product in this reaction. The balanced equation for this reaction is:

$2Al_2O_3 + \text{heat} \rightarrow 4Al + 3O_2$

If you heat 50.0 grams of aluminum ore, and the reaction is completed, how many grams of pure aluminum will you get?

21.1 Classifying Reactions

Question: How can you predict the products in a reaction?

In this Investigation, you will:

1 Predict the products in a double-displacement reaction.

2 Deduce the rules for solubility of an ionic compound.

A double-displacement reaction is a chemical reaction in which the ions from the two reactants change places. One of the new compounds formed is sometimes insoluble and forms a cloudy precipitate. In this Investigation, you will develop a set of rules for solubility that will allow you to make predictions about the solubility of the products of double-displacement reactions.

Safety Tip: Wear goggles and an apron during the Investigation.

1 Writing the chemical formulas of the reactants

Write the chemical formulas for the compounds you will react (Table 19.2 on page 327 of the Student Edition).

compound	positive ion	column of periodic table (if monoatomic)	negative ion	chemical formula
ammonium hydroxide				
calcium chloride				
magnesium sulfate				
sodium chloride				
sodium hydroxide				
sodium phosphate				

2 Deducing your rules for solubility - part I

All of the compounds in the table above are soluble. You know this because the solutions you have in front of you are clear. Rules for the solubility of ionic compounds have to do with the combination of positive and negative ions. The solubility of ionic compounds also has to do with the group on the periodic table which the positive ion comes from. For example, one rule you could deduce from the table is:

If an element from Group I is the positive ion and a phosphate is the negative ion, then the compound is soluble.

Write your rules on a separate sheet of paper. You may include the rule above.

3   ## Determining products and writing the equations

For each pair of reactants in the table below: (1)Write the possible products into the middle column; (2)Put a few drops of each reactant into a small beaker or spot plate and observe the reaction; and (c)Note whether or not a precipitate has formed as a result of the reaction.

reactants	possible products	precipitate? yes or no
$CaCl_2$ + NaOH		
$CaCl_2$ + Na_3PO_4		
NaOH + Na_3PO_4		
NaCl + NH_4OH		
NaOH + $MgSO_4$		
Na_3PO_4 + $MgSO_4$		
$MgSO_4$ + $CaCl_2$		
$CaCl_2$ + NH_4OH		
NaCl + $MgSO_4$		
NH_4OH + $MgSO_4$		

4   ## Finalizing your solubility rules

1   Look at the rules you wrote before and circle all of the products above that you know are soluble.
2   Identify the products that you absolutely know are the precipitates.
3   Based on your findings, add additional rules to your list.

5   ## Applying your rules

Now that you have your own rules for determining solubility, predict the precipitate for the reactions your teacher writes on the board.

21.2 Energy in Reactions

Question: How can you classify reactions based on energy?

In this Investigation, you will:

1 Measure energy changes in three different reactions.
2 Determine whether the reaction is exothermic or endothermic.
3 Write complete balanced equations that show the energy changes in each reaction.

You know that when a chemical reaction occurs, chemical bonds are broken in the reactants to make new products. Breaking bonds requires energy. Energy is released when new products are formed. In **endothermic reactions**, more energy is required to break the bonds in the reactants than is given off when the products are formed. In **exothermic reactions**, more energy is given off when new products are formed than is required to break the bonds in the reactants. In this Investigation, you will measure the energy changes in reactions and categorize the reactions as endothermic or exothermic.

Safety Tip: Wear goggles and an apron for this Investigation

1 Measuring energy changes in reactions

You will use a thermometer to measure energy changes in each reaction.

In each reaction, it is important that you measure and record the temperature of the liquid in the beaker before you add another substance.

After you add a substance, record the highest or lowest temperature you observe.

a. What does a change in temperature tell you about the energy in a reaction?
b. If a reaction occurs and no temperature change can be measured, what might that indicate about the reaction?

2 Reaction #1 Dissolution of ammonium nitrate

Reaction notes: When an ionic compound dissolves in water, the ionic bonds in the compound dissolve and the ions are released into the solution. This type of reaction is called **dissolution**. In this reaction, ammonium nitrate is the ionic compound that dissolves into its positive and negative ions. Follow the steps below to complete the reaction. Record all observations in your notebook.

1 Obtain a 250 milliliter beaker containing 200 milliliters of water.
2 Measure the temperature of the water and record it in your notebook.
3 Add 30 grams of ammonium nitrate to the beaker.
4 Stir with a stirring rod and immerse the thermometer in the solution.
5 Record the highest or lowest temperature you observe in your notebook.
6 Record any other observations you make in your notebook.

3   ## Reaction #2 Decomposition of hydrogen peroxide

Reaction notes: A **decomposition reaction** occurs when one compound decomposes to form two or more products. Follow the steps below to complete the reaction. Record all observations in your notebook.

1   Obtain a 250 milliliter beaker and add 150 milliliters of hydrogen peroxide to the beaker.
2   Measure the temperature of the hydrogen peroxide and record it in your notebook.
3   Place a slice of potato in the beaker.
4   Immerse the thermometer into the beaker with the potato.
5   Record the highest or lowest temperature you observe in your notebook.

4   ## Reaction #3 Dissolution of calcium chloride

Reaction notes: When calcium chloride is added to water, it dissolves into its positive and negative ions. This is another dissolution reaction. Follow the steps below and record your observations in your notebook.

1   Obtain a 250 milliliter beaker containing 200 milliliters of water.
2   Measure the temperature of the water and record it in your notebook
3   Add 30.0 grams of calcium chloride to the beaker.
4   Stir with a stirring rod and immerse the thermometer in the solution.
5   Record the highest or lowest temperature you observe in your notebook.

5   ## Classifying the reactions and showing energy changes

For each reaction you just observed, indicate whether it is exothermic or endothermic, based on your observations. Next, write the balanced equation for each reaction. Indicate energy changes in each reaction by following the example below.

$$2H_2 + O_2 + energy \longrightarrow 2H_2O$$

Is this an example of an exothermic or endothermic reaction?

rxn	type of reaction (exothermic or endothermic)	Write the complete, balanced equation. Show energy changes in your equation.
#1		
#2		
#3		

22.1   Nuclear Reactions

Question: How do you simulate nuclear decay?

In this Investigation, you will:

1   Investigate the concept of nuclear decay.

2   Graph your data and interpret your results.

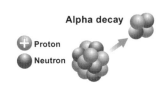

With 92 protons and 146 neutrons, the nucleus of uranium-238 has a tendency to fall apart or "decay" because it is **unstable**. In other words, the nucleus of a uranium-238 atom is **radioactive**. It emits **radiation** in the forms of particles and energy until it becomes an atom with a more stable nucleus. In this case, uranium-238 emits an alpha particle to become a thorium-234 atom. An alpha particle is composed of two protons and two neutrons.

Eventually, uranium-238 decays naturally to lead-206 which is not radioactive. The time for half of the atoms in a sample of uranium-238 to perform this entire nuclear decay process takes about 4.5 billion years! In other words, the half-life of uranium-238 is 4.5 billion years. In this Investigation, you will learn more about half-life and simulate the radioactive decay of a new element.

1   Discussing radioactivity

Your teacher has given you a can of pennies to represent the atoms of a sample of a newly discovered, radioactive element. Discuss the following with your group. Record your answers in your notebook.

a.   With your group, decide on a name for your element.

b.   Why is your element radioactive? What does this tell you about its nucleus?

c.   Since your element is radioactive, what is happening to its nucleus?

d.   If this were a real radioactive element, what precautions would you have to take? Why?

2   Making a prediction

You will use the pennies that you have been given to simulate the process of radioactive decay. When you have completed the simulation, you will construct a graph of your data. Sample number will be on the x-axis, and number of decayed atoms per sample will be on the y-axis. What do you think this graph will look like? Sketch your prediction in your lab notebook. Reading over step 3 (Simulating the process of radioactive decay) will help you make this prediction.

3   Simulating the process of radioactive decay

To simulate the process of radioactive decay follow the steps of the procedure below.

1   Shake your can of pennies and spill them out onto a tray or table.

2   Remove all pennies that are "heads" up and count them.

3   Record these as decayed atoms in Table 1 on the next page.

4   Put the rest of the pennies back into the can, shake them again.

5 Spill them out onto the tray or table, and again, remove and count the "heads."

6 Repeat this process until you have no more pennies left.

7 If necessary, add extra rows to your table.

4 Recording the data

Table 1: Data from the experiment

sample number	number of decayed atoms	sample number	number of decayed atoms
1		8	
2		9	
3		10	
4		11	
5		12	
6		13	
7		14	

5   Graphing your data

Graph your data for number of decayed atoms per sample vs. sample number. Label the axes clearly. Be sure to provide a title for the graph. Be sure to use the entire graph in plotting your data. Use the graph paper provided by your teacher.

6 Interpreting your graph

Respond to the following in your lab notebook.

a. Write a paragraph that describes what your graph looks like.

b. What part of this simulation represents the half-life of this new element? Explain your answer.

c. If the half-life of your element was 430 years and you had 2000 atoms of this element, how long would it take for the element to undergo complete radioactive decay to a stable isotope? What year would it be when the element finished decaying? Note: As you work through this problem, round the number of atoms left to a whole number. For example, round 62.5 to 63.

7 Wrapping up

a. Were you correct in your prediction for what your graph would look like?

b. Make a list of pros and a list of cons regarding the uses of radioactive elements. Each list should have at least three points. As you make your lists, think about how radioactive elements are used today. You may need to do research on the Internet or in your library to make your lists.

22.2 Carbon Reactions

Question: How do your choices impact the environment?

In this Investigation, you will:

1 Use consumer information to make environmentally conscious and economically responsible decisions.

2 Understand the environmental effects of using fossil fuels.

If you needed to buy a car to drive to school or work, what kind of car would you buy?

In this Investigation, you will use consumer information to evaluate how your answer to this question might affect the environment and your personal finances. For example, you will calculate how much carbon dioxide your car produces. You will also learn how the sun's energy may be used to reduce carbon dioxide in the atmosphere.

1 Choosing a car or truck

1 Prior to the Investigation, choose the car or truck you would buy to drive to work or school each day. Find three facts that justify your choice. Make a brochure that describes your car. Include the facts and any photographs, magazine clippings or articles you find.

2 Use the ACEEE's Green Book -- The Environmental Guide to Cars and Trucks or the Internet (http://greenercars.org/indexplus.html) to find the fuel economy for your car or truck for highway and city driving. Write this information in your notebook. The unit for fuel economy is miles per gallon of gasoline (MPG).

3 Figure out how many gallons of gasoline you will need to drive 500 miles in the city and 500 miles on the highway.

4 Use the price per gallon of gas provided by your teacher to calculate how much money you need to buy enough gasoline for your car or truck to travel 500 miles in the city and 500 miles on the highway.

2 The environmental effects

a. You will use the combustion reaction for iso-octane to find out how much carbon dioxide (CO_2) your car produces. The equation for the combustion of iso-octane is:
$$2C_8H_{18}\,(l) + 25O_2(g) \text{-->} 16CO_2\,(g) + 18H_2O\,(g) + 10{,}9000kJ.$$
From this equation, you can tell that you would need 2 moles of iso-octane and 25 moles of oxygen to get a complete combustion reaction that produces 10,900 kilojoules of energy.

b. Calculate the formula masses of iso-octane and CO_2. Use the periodic table to help you.

c. Calculate the mass of one gallon of iso-octane. The density of iso-octane is 0.69 g/ml. One gallon is equivalent to 3840 ml.

d. Calculate the mass of CO_2 that will be produced to drive 500 miles in the city and 500 miles on the highway. Use the following formula:

$$\frac{\text{mass of iso-octane needed to travel 500 miles}}{\text{(formula mass of iso-octane} \times 2)} = \frac{\text{mass of carbon dioxide produced after 500 miles}}{\text{(formula mass of carbon dioxide} \times 16)}$$

3 | ## Using the sun's energy

All plants use photosynthesis to convert the sun's energy into chemical energy. Unlike combustion which is exothermic, photosynthesis is endothermic and requires energy. The chemical equation for photosynthesis is:

$$6CO_2 + 6H_2O + 2870 \text{ kJ} \rightarrow C_6H_{12}O_6 + 6O_2.$$

Through photosynthesis, plants assimilate the carbon in CO_2 into their tissues. In this way, photosynthesis does contribute to reducing CO_2 in the atmosphere. For this Investigation, assume that one tree converts 32 pounds of CO_2 to glucose ($C_6H_{12}O_6$) each year. This figure is equivalent to 14.545 kilograms or 14,545 grams of CO_2.

a. Figure out how many trees you would need to plant to offset the amount of CO_2 your car or truck produces each year for driving 500 miles in the city and 500 miles on the highway.

4 | ## Evaluating choices

Use the data from the whole class to make a list of the top five cars and trucks in each category.

a. The best fuel economy for driving in the city.
b. The best fuel economy for driving on the highway.
c. The worst fuel economy for driving in the city.
d. The worst fuel economy for driving on the highway.
e. The least carbon dioxide produced each year.
f. The most carbon dioxide produced each year.

5 | ## Reaching conclusions

Respond to the following in your lab notebook.

a. Was your car in any of the top five lists? If so, which one?
b. On a scale of 1 - 5, rate the fuel economy of your car or truck. A "1" means your car is not fuel efficient and a "5" means that your car or truck is very fuel efficient. Explain your rating choice.
c. On a scale of 1 - 5, rate your car or truck according to how much carbon dioxide it produces. A "5" means that your car or truck produces a great deal of carbon dioxide. Explain your answer.
d.   Go back to the three reasons that you chose your car or truck. Have your three reasons changed because of this Investigation? Give at least one new reason for selecting or not selecting your car or truck. Explain your answer.
e. What are the consequences of having too much carbon dioxide in the atmosphere?
f. Is it reasonable to say that we can plant trees to compensate for all the carbon dioxide we produce? Why or why not?

What is a Solution?

Question: Can you identify mixtures as solutions, suspensions, or colloids?

In this Investigation, you will:

1   Use what you know about solutions, suspensions, and colloids to categorize six mixtures.
2   Observe the Tyndall effect.

 In your reading, you learned about solutions, suspensions, and colloids. A table on page 395 of the Student Edition summarizes the characteristics of these mixtures. The Tyndall effect is one way to distinguish between solutions and colloids. In this Investigation, you will construct an apparatus to view the Tyndall effect.

1   Preparing the Tyndall effect viewer

⬥ 👓 ▮ **Safety Tips: Wear safety goggles and an apron throughout the experiment. Use a utility knife with care.**

1   Line the shoe box with black paper.

2   In the center of one of the long sides, cut a 3-by-3-centimeter square with scissors or a utility knife. The bottom edge of the square should be 5 centimeters from the bottom of the box.

3   In the center of one of the short sides, cut another 3-by-3-centimeter square. The bottom edge of this square should also be 5 centimeters from the bottom of the box.

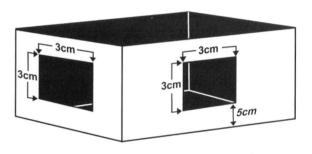

2   Testing the Tyndall effect viewer

1   Fill a clear glass 250-milliliter beaker with 200 milliliters of water. Grind the chalk (calcium carbonate) to a powder in your mortar and pestle. Mix about 2 grams of powdered chalk into the water. This is your colloid test solution. Place the beaker in the center of the box and close the lid.

2   Place a flashlight against the square cut in the long side of the box. Shine the light into the box.

3   View the beaker through the square cut in the short side. The path of the light beam should be visible in your mixture. In your lab notebook, describe what you see.

4   Fill a 250-milliliter beaker with 200 milliliters of water. Place it in the viewer. Can you see the path of the light beam now? If no beam is visible, the viewer is working correctly.

3   Preparing the mixtures

1   Fill six 250-milliliter glass beakers with 200 milliliters each of water. Stir one of the following substances into each of five beakers. One beaker will contain only water.

  (1) 40 milliliters corn oil; (2) 6 drops of food coloring; (3) 2.5 grams corn starch; (4) 9 grams of granulated sugar; (5) 3 grams modeling clay.

2   Label your beakers so that you remember which mixture is in each one.

3   [hand icon] For mixture (6), carefully heat 200 milliliters water to 100 °C. Using a hot pad, pour it into a 250-milliliter heat-resistant glass beaker. Add 2.5 grams plain gelatin. Stir the mixture.

4   Designing your procedure

a.   Revisit the table of characteristics of solutions, colloids, and suspensions in the Student Edition (page 395). Design a procedure that will enable you to classify your six mixtures correctly. Your procedure should include at least two tests for each mixture.

b.   Record your procedure in your lab notebook.

c.   Observe each mixture. In your lab notebook, write a hypothesis that explains what type of mixture you believe it is. Give a reason for each prediction.

5   Collecting your data

Follow your written procedure. Record your results in the table below.

Substance added to 200 mL water	results of test #1	results of test #2	solution, colloid, or suspension?
(1) corn oil			
(2) food coloring			
(3) corn starch			
(4) granulated sugar			
(5) modeling clay			
(6) gelatin			
(7) plain water			control solution

6   [cup icon] Cleaning up

1   Solutions and colloids may be washed down a sink. Clean and dry the beakers.

2   Use a coffee filter to separate the solid particles out of any suspensions. Solids may be thrown in a wastebasket. Liquids may be washed down a sink. Clean and dry the beakers.

7   What are your conclusions?

Record your answers to these questions in your lab notebook.

a.   Did your procedures help you tell the difference between solutions, colloids and suspensions? Provide evidence to support your response.

b.   Were your hypotheses about each mixture correct? If not, explain why.

c.   Why was plain water tested in the Investigation? What does the word *control* mean?

d.   Is water a true solution? Explain your answer.

e.   If you had a mixture that was not translucent, how could you determine if it should be classified as a solution, colloid, or suspension?

Dissolving Rate

Question: How can you influence dissolving rates?

In this Investigation, you will:

1 Design three methods for dissolving rock salt in water.
2 Calculate the dissolving rate obtained by each method.
3 Propose the fastest possible method you can imagine for dissolving rock salt in water.

What are the factors that influence how fast a substance will dissolve? Now you have the opportunity to design an experiment in which you test the effectiveness of three different methods of dissolving rock salt in water. You may be familiar with rock salt as a substance that is used in ice cream churns.

1 Guidelines for your experiment

You will design three different methods for dissolving rock salt in water. For each method, you will write a procedure. Your procedures and experiments must follow the guidelines listed below.

- You will start with approximately 5 grams of rock salt. Place whole crystals on the balance until you have as close to 5 grams as possible. You may NOT break any crystals to obtain exactly 5 grams. Record the exact mass in Table 1 (on the next page).

- You will use a graduated cylinder to measure 250 milliliters of room temperature water. Pour it into a 500-milliliter beaker or glass jar with a lid (your choice).

- You will start timing as soon as the rock salt is added to the water.

- You will follow your written procedure for getting the rock salt to enter the solution. Timing ends when all the rock salt appears to have entered the solution.

- You will calculate the dissolving rate in units of grams per second. For example, if it took 150 seconds for 5 grams of rock salt to enter the solution, the dissolving rate would be 5 grams / 150 seconds or 0.033 grams / second.

2 Brainstorming ideas and formulating your hypothesis

a. As a group, decide on three different methods to influence the rate of dissolving. Remember that in order to draw valid conclusions in an experiment, you can change only one variable at a time! In your lab notebook, write a step-by-step procedure for each method. When you have finished, submit your set of procedures to your teacher for approval.

b. In your lab notebook, write a statement describing which of your three procedures will produce the fastest dissolving rate. Be sure to explain your reasoning.

◆ **Be sure to include safety instructions in your procedures.**

3   Collecting your data

Follow your written procedure for each of your three methods, recording your data and observations in Table 1 each time.

1   Write a short description of each procedure in the first column of Table 1.

2   Record the amount of rock salt used for each procedure in the second column.

3   While you conduct each procedure, note any observations, problems, or changes to the procedure in the fifth column.

4   The time for dissolving the rock salt and your calculation for the dissolving rate will be recorded in the third and fourth columns.

When you have finished this part of the Investigation, clean all of the materials used by your group.

Table 1: Dissolving rate procedures and data

Summary of procedure	amount of rock salt (grams)	time to dissolve rock salt (seconds)	dissolving rate (grams / second)	notes

4   What did you learn?

Record the answers to the following questions in your lab notebook.

a.   Using what you have learned in your reading, describe what was happening on a molecular level as you tried to dissolve the rock salt. You may want to use diagrams in your explanation.

b.   Which method produced the fastest dissolving rate? Did you prove or disprove your hypothesis?

c.   What other, even faster, methods could you use to get 5 grams of rock salt to dissolve in 250 milliliters of water? Describe these.

Solubility

Question: How does temperature affect solubility?

In this Investigation, you will:

1 Observe how temperature influences dissolving rate.

2 Develop an explanation for how temperature influences solubility.

Have you ever tried to get sugar to dissolve in a drink? You may know that you can get the job done more easily if the liquid is hot rather than cold. But why is this the case? In this Investigation, you will observe how temperature influences the dissolving rate of a sugar cube in water. Based on your observations, you will come up with a set of ideas for how temperature influences solubility.

1 **Introduction to the experiment**

You will observe individual sugar cubes dissolving in water at different temperatures. For each temperature, you will watch the cubes dissolve. Because you will not stir the water, the sugar cubes will not completely dissolve during this part of the Investigation. Instead, the cubes will fall apart and become small piles of sugar at the bottom of the beakers. When one sugar cube has fallen apart and partially dissolved, you will add another one to that particular beaker. Record your data in Tables 1, 2 and 3 on the next page. Record your responses, notes and observations in your lab notebook.

2 **Procedure**

⬙ 🧤 Safety Tip: Carefully follow your teacher's directions for working with the hot water. Take care not to spill it on yourself or others.

1 Obtain 10 sugar cubes, three beakers, three styrofoam cups and a water soluble marker. Use the water soluble marker to color one face of each of three sugar cubes.

2 One beaker and one styrofoam cup will be used for each water temperature. Label the cups and beakers: "ice," "room temperature," and "hot." Place one sugar cube in each beaker with the colored side facing up.

3 Obtain ice, room temperature, and hot water in your labeled styrofoam cups. Measure the temperature of the water in each cup. Record these starting temperatures in Table 1.

4 Gently transfer the water from the styrofoam cups to each of the beakers. Fill the beakers to the 50-milliliter mark with the water from the cups. *Do not disturb the cubes as you fill each beaker.*

5 Record this time as the starting time for the experiment in Table 2. Record the time in hours, minutes and seconds.

6 First, observe how the ink from the faces of the sugar cube dissolves in the water at each temperature. Record your observations in your lab notebook.

7 Observe how the sugar cubes dissolve in each of the three beakers. Watch the cubes from the sides and tops of the beakers. Record your observations in your lab notebook. Answer these questions: (a) What happens to the color on the sugar cube? (b) What happens to a sugar cube as it dissolves? and (c) What does the water above the sugar cube look like?

8   When all that is left of a cube is a small pile of sugar, write the time in Table 3. Record the time in hours, minutes and seconds. Then, carefully add another cube to that beaker. The second and third cubes added to beakers will not have colored faces.

9   Repeat step 8 until at least one of the beakers has three collapsed sugar cubes. There will be three small piles of sugar at the bottom of this beaker. At this point, the experiment has ended. Record the ending time in Table 2.

10 Record the ending water temperature for each beaker in Table 1.

11 Gently swirl each of the beakers three times so that the sugar on the bottom is stirred up. What do you notice about the water above the sugar? Record your observations in your lab notebook.

Table 1: Starting and ending temperatures for the experiment

Temperature range	Starting temperature (°C)	Ending temperature (°C)
Ice water		
Room temperature water		
Hot water		

Table 2: Starting and ending times for the experiment

Start time for experiment hour:minute:second	End time for experiment hour:minute:second

Table 3: Sugar cube data

Number of cubes	Time recorded when cube dissolves in ice water	Time recorded when cube dissolves in room temperature water	Time recorded when cube dissolves in hot water
1			
2			
3			

3   Analyzing your results

a. In which beaker of water did three sugar cubes dissolve the fastest? In which beaker of water did the sugar cubes dissolve the slowest?

b. Did the ice water stay colder than the room temperature water for the whole experiment? Did the hot water stay warmer than the room temperature water for the whole experiment? Why was it important to check the water temperature in each beaker at the start and at the end of the experiment?

4   Drawing conclusions

a. List three observations you made during the experiment. Use what you know about solubility to explain each of these observations. In other words, describe why something you observed occurred or looked a certain way.

b. Based on your observations of the experiment and your own ideas, draw a diagram that shows how temperature influences how a substance dissolves on the molecular level.

Water

Question: What is the quality of your tap water?

In this Investigation, you will:

1   Learn about the composition of tap water.
2   Learn and use basic water quality tests.

If you were to take a trip across the United States, you might notice that water in different places doesn't taste the same. Why is that? The taste of water has to do with where it comes from and then how it is treated by a municipal water company before it comes out of a faucet. The taste also depends on whether or not water contains dissolved minerals from sediment in the ground or from pipes in the plumbing system. What does your water taste like? Where does it originate before it reaches the treatment plant? This Investigation will show you simple tests you can use to better understand your tap water.

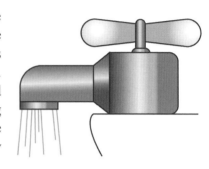

1 Obtaining your water samples

1   Before coming to class, collect two 500-milliliter (about 2 cups) samples of water from a faucet at your house. One sample should be of very hot water and the other sample very cold water.

2   Collect your samples in large sealable plastic bags. Be sure to label which bag has the cold sample and which the hot sample. Let the water run for 5 minutes before collecting each of your samples. Once you have your samples, place them inside a **second** larger, sealable bag. Make sure all the bags are tightly sealed! You will have to be very careful while you transport your samples. Drop them off with your teacher when you arrive at school.

3   ★ **Try to use the water that runs from the faucet before you collect your sample. For example, you can collect it for watering your houseplants.**

4   While you are at home collecting your samples, look for any signs that you may have high levels of copper (blue stains), iron (orange stains), or minerals in your water (scale on glasses). Write down your observations in your lab notebook.

5   Find out where your water comes from. You may need to use the Internet to trace this information. A helpful Web site is http://www.epa.gov/surf.

2 Testing your water quality

For each of the following water quality tests, you will be pouring about 20 milliliters of your samples into small, clear beakers. You will need two clean beakers for each test. For each test, record the results in your lab notebook.

👓 🧪 **Safety Tip: Wear goggles and a lab apron while performing the tests. When you have completed all the tests, be sure to wash your hands.**

The pH test: The pH of your tap water can have an effect on the pipes in your house. The pH scale ranges from acids (0 to 6) to bases (8 to 14). Pure water is neither an acid or a base. It is neutral (pH of 7). Acids can corrode pipes and cause iron, copper, or lead to get into your drinking water. Bases can mean that calcium or magnesium deposits will clog your pipes.

a. Add a pH wide-range tablet to each of your samples.

b. Compare your results with the color series that your teacher has set up. What color is each sample?

c. What is the pH of each of your samples?

The hardness test: Hard water has high levels of dissolved calcium and magnesium. These minerals form white deposits on drinking glasses and inside pipes. The deposits, called "scale," can clog pipes.

a. Add a hardness-test tablet to each of your samples.

b. Compare your results with the color series that you teacher has set up. What color is each sample?

c. Is the water in each of your samples hard or soft?

The chlorine test: Chlorine in safe amounts is added by water treatment facilities to kill harmful bacteria and algae. Chlorine does not occur naturally in water supplies.

a. Add a chlorine-test tablet to each of your samples.

b. Compare your results with the color series that your teacher has set up. What color is each sample?

c. Do your samples contain low or high amounts of chlorine?

The iron test: Iron is a natural component of tap water. However, when water is too acidic, iron may be leached from pipes into the water supply.

a. Add an iron-test tablet to each of your samples.

b. Compare your results with the color series that your teacher has set up. What color is each sample?

c. Do your samples contain low or high amounts of iron?
    NOTE: Iron is unstable in water. For this reason, you may not detect iron even when it is present in your water supply.

The copper test: Copper, like iron, can be leached from pipes into the water supply when the water is too acidic. In small quantities, copper is an essential element for human health. Too much copper can make water taste bitter and cause blue stains in sinks and bathtubs.

a. Add a copper-test tablet to each of your samples.

b. Compare your results with the color series that your teacher set up. What color is each sample?

c. Do your samples contain low or high amounts of copper or none at all?

3   Analyzing results and drawing conclusions

a. Organize your results into a table.

b. Write a five to eight sentence paragraph that explains the results of your testing.

c. Is there a difference between the hot and cold tap water samples? Why or why not?

d. How could the method of testing water quality that was used in this Investigation be improved?

e. At a local store or in your classroom, look at the packaging for a water-filtration device. What substances -- and how much of their total presence in the water -- does the device claim to remove? Based on your testing results, would you purchase this device to improve the quality of your own drinking water? Explain your answer.

24.2 The Water Cycle

Question: What is the quality of your local surface water?

In this Investigation, you will:

1 Meet a specialist in the field of water quality testing.

2 Visit a local surface water area and perform water quality testing.

Water is one of our most important natural resources. Consequently, many careers involve studying and taking care of our water supply. Some scientists test and monitor the water supply and some study weather patterns to better understand the water cycle. People involved in government agencies, nonprofit organizations, and the media keep track of information about water and make this information available to the general public. In this Investigation, you will meet a specialist in the field of water quality testing, and perform water quality tests. As you complete the Investigation, think about what causes water pollution. What actions can you take to reduce your water usage and to affect water quality?

1 Meeting a water quality specialist

a. Before you meet the specialist, write down his or her name and occupation. Prepare three questions that you would like to ask the specialist.

b. During the meeting, take notes. Review your notes and write down at least three new things that you learned from the specialist.

2 Preparing for your field trip

As you prepare for the field trip, be sure to write down your work in your lab notebook. On your own:

1 Complete section 24.2 on pages 415-421 of the Student Edition. This section briefly describes the procedure and tests for water quality testing.

2 Familiarize yourself with the testing procedures for performing the water quality testing. Each test involves some special steps. Additionally, the field trip will be more enjoyable if you understand the tests and how they are performed.

With your group:

1 Describe the place that your class will perform water quality testing. Where is it located? What kind of surface water will be tested?

2 Make a prediction about the quality of the surface water to be tested. Will the water in this location be clean or polluted? Justify your answer.

With the class:

1   Create data sheets for collecting quantitative and qualitative data. What information needs to go on the data sheets?

2   Look at a map of the surface water that will be tested. Discuss and decide where samples will be taken. Assign locations to each group.

3   ## Field trip: testing surface water

👓 **Safety Tip: Wear goggles while you perform the coliform test and the tests for phosphate and nitrate. Be sure to wash your hands when you have completed the tests.**

1   Make general observations about the surface water and the day's weather.

2   Follow your data sheets for recording information at each sampling sight.

3   You will be using supplies from a water quality testing kit to perform this Investigation. Be sure to follow the directions for using these supplies while you perform the tests.

4   ## Follow up

a.   With your group, go over your data sheets carefully and make sure that you have recorded all the observations that you wanted to make.

b.   Compile the data with the class. Make tables of the data for each test.

c.   Using the data for each test, each group should create a water quality report for the surface water tested. Be sure to address whether or not the quality of the water at this site matched your prediction.

d.   In your report, include a section that addresses what your class can do to maintain the water quality at the test site or help improve the water quality at the test site.

25.1 Acids, Bases, and pH

Question: What is pH?

In this Investigation, you will:

1   Make a pH scale by creating a pH indicator with chemicals of known pH.

2   Use the pH scale to figure out the pH of additional chemicals.

3   Use the pH of a "mystery" chemical to help you identify it.

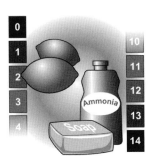

Life exists inside a certain range of pH numbers. A pH value describes whether a solution is acidic, basic (alkaline), or neutral. Acids are solutions that contain a majority of H+ ions, and bases (or alkalis) are solutions that contain a majority of OH- ions. Neutral solutions have equal numbers of H+ and OH- ions.

In this Investigation, you will learn the pH of several everyday solutions. As you measure pH of these solutions, see if you can determine some properties of acids and some properties of bases.

1 Setting up

1   Collect the following materials: spot plates, permanent marker, eyedroppers or pipettes, 5 milliliters of red cabbage juice (a pH indicator), red and blue litmus paper (pH indicators). Additionally, collect 2 milliliters each of the solutions listed in the data table (solutions 1 to 12).

2   Record your data, observations and responses in your lab notebook during the Investigation.

Safety Tip: Wear goggles and a lab apron during the Investigation to protect your eyes and clothing from the household chemicals that you will be using.

2 Make a pH scale using indicators

1   To create your pH scale, you will be using solutions 1 to 7 in the table below. Place the following labels for these solutions **in order** on a spot plate. If you don't have seven wells in a row on one spot plate, place two plates side by side. The labels should describe the solution and its pH.

Lemon, pH 2   Vinegar, 3   Soda water, 4   Red cabbage juice (the control), 6.5

Baking soda, 8.5   Hand soap, 10   Ammonia, 11

2   Using a pipette, place three drops of red cabbage juice in each of the seven labeled wells.

3   Using a pipette, add two drops of each of the solutions to the appropriately labeled well. Use a different eyedropper or pipette for each solution. However, if you must use the same dropper or pipette, thoroughly rinse it in fresh water after each solution before using it for a new solution. Record the color changes in your data table. The color series you see on the plate(s) represents a pH scale. We will refer to it as the **pH test plate**. You will use it to identify the pH of other solutions.

4   Dip the red litmus paper and the blue litmus paper into each well of the pH test plate. Record the results according to the directions in the data table.

Name of solution	Color when mixed with red cabbage juice	Red litmus paper: If paper turns blue, write "base," or make an "x"	Blue litmus paper: If paper turns red, write "acid," or make an "x"	pH
1. lemon				2
2. vinegar				3
3. seltzer				4
4. red cabbage juice				6.5
5. baking soda solution				8.5
6. hand soap solution				10
7. ammonia				11
8. green tea				
9. antibacterial cleaner				
10. apple juice				
11. mystery solution A				
12. mystery solution B				

3 Evaluating the role of the pH test plate

a. What is the role of a pH indicator? What is the range of pH measured by each indicator (red cabbage juice, red litmus paper, blue litmus paper)?

b. Which of your solutions has the highest concentration of H+ ions? Which has the highest concentration of OH- ions? Explain your reasoning.

c. The red cabbage juice used in the Investigations has two roles. It is the pH indicator and, in the series on the pH test plate, it is a *control*. Why is a control needed on the pH test plate?

4 Using pH indicators to measure unknown pH

1 Repeat steps 2.2 to 2.4 for solutions 8 to 12: Use another spot plate for these five solutions. The labels should describe the solution. At this point, you do not know the pH of these solutions.

2 Identify the pH of solutions 8 to 12: Compare the color reactions and the litmus paper results for solutions 8 to 12 with the pH test plate. Determine the pH of these solutions using this data.

5 Identifying mystery solutions

Mystery solutions A and B are identical to two other solutions you used in this lab. Use your results to identify these solutions. What is the identity of mystery solution A? What is the identity of mystery B? List evidence to support your claims.

6 What did you learn?

a. List the pros and cons of using red cabbage juice and litmus paper as pH indicators.

b. Various professions use pH indicators. For example, photographers use stop bath in developing, and swimming pools are maintained using information from pH indicators. Find out how these pH indicators work in these (or other) situations, and what the color changes mean.

Acid Rain

Question: What is acid rain?

In this Investigation, you will:

1　Learn about the biology of the water flea (Daphnia).
2　Observe the effects of different concentrations (dilutions) of acid on Daphnia.
3　Learn about acid rain and its effects on organisms in aquatic environments.

Under normal circumstances, the pH of ponds and lakes ranges from 6 to 8. When a pond or lake has experienced acid rain events, the pH may be lowered. At a pH value less than 5.6, numerous organisms in the pond are harmed. In this Investigation, you will be simulating the effects of acid rain on a common pond and lake organism, the water flea (Daphnia). Daphnia is a small transparent organism that is related to crabs and shrimp. In ponds and lakes this organism serves as a food source for small fish and the larvae of larger organisms. If any environmental effect harms the population of Daphnia, what do you think would happen to the other organisms in the pond or lake?

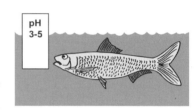

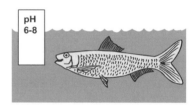

1　Observing Daphnia

Obtain a culture vial and some wide-bore pipettes. Each vial has at least six Daphnia individuals.

a.　To understand how Daphnia might react to an acidic environment, it is best to figure out how it acts under normal conditions. Look carefully at this organism. Draw a detailed diagram of a single individual. It may help to use a magnifying glass to see the different parts of this small animal.

b.　Once you have drawn your diagram, watch the Daphnia individuals for 5 minutes. Record the movements and behaviors of Daphnia in your lab notebook. Be very detailed in your recording.

c.　Based on your observations, name the parts of Daphnia that you included in your diagram. Next to your label, write what you think the role of each part is.

2　Making predictions

You will be exposing Daphnia to different concentrations of the weak acid vinegar dissolved in water. In your lab notebook, record what you think will happen as you expose Daphnia to vinegar. Include a list of behaviors that you think will indicate that Daphnia is being harmed by the acid. Using what you know about pH, harmful pH levels, and the pH of vinegar (measured in Investigation 25.1) determine the lowest concentration of vinegar that you think will cause harm to Daphnia. Record this hypothesis.

3　Simulating the effect of acid rain on Daphnia

1　Your teacher will give you five vinegar treatment solutions (each is a different concentration, or *dilution*, of vinegar). These treatments are listed on the table below as the ratio of volume of vinegar to volume of distilled water. For example, the 1:50 treatment has one part vinegar to 50 parts of distilled water. (The word part refers to a certain amount of liquid.) You will also have a control treatment of distilled water (DiH_2O). You will be using distilled water throughout the Investigation because the chlorine in tap water would kill Daphnia.

2   When you are ready to tests the effects of acid on Daphnia, remove the lid from the culture vial. Use a wide-bore pipette to transfer a single Daphnia from the culture vial to the control vial of DiH_2O. Additionally, transfer another Daphnia from the culture vial to the 1:5000 vial. Record the start time (the hour and minute) in the table below. Place the lids back on the vials.

3   Begin observing the effect of the DiH_2O and the 1:5000 treatment immediately. Compare the movements of the single Daphnia in the DiH_2O vial with the single Daphnia in the 1:5000 treatment. Record your observations in your lab notebook.

4   Observe the two vials for 2 minutes. If the Daphnia dies in the 1:5000 treatment, record the time that this happens. If the Daphnia does not die during this time, keep observing the vial. Continue to keep time on this vial, but continue with the rest of the experiment.

5   Repeat steps 3.2 to 3.4 for the next four treatments. Compare Daphnia in the treatments with Daphnia in the control vial. Record your observations and keep time.

6   The end time for any treatment is the point at which a Daphnia individual dies in the treatment.

7   When 30 minutes have past since the first start time that you recorded, this part of the Investigation ends. In the Comments column of the data table, record the status of the Daphnia for each vial.

8   Using pH paper or indicator tablets to figure out the pH of each treatment solution and the DiH_2O control. Record the pH value for these in the table below.

Control and Treatments (vinegar: DiH_2O)	pH	Start time	Comments	End time
DiH_2O				
1:50				
1:100				
1:500				
1:1000				
1:5000				

4   Analyzing results and drawing conclusions

a.   Write a paragraph that summarizes the results of this simulation experiment. Do not include any conclusions in this paragraph. Simply write down what you observed.

b.   Write a paragraph that explains whether or not your predictions from step 2 were correct. Include a conclusion statement that addresses what you learned by performing this simulation experiment.

c.   What does the word simulation mean? Was this experiment a good way to understand some of the effects of acid rain on organisms that live in a pond or lake? Explain your answer.

d.   What does the word ecosystem mean? Why is it difficult to simulate the effects of an event like acid rain on an ecosystem?

e.   Write up this simulation experiment as a lab report. Follow the format provided to you by your teacher.

Temperature Scales

Question: How is temperature measured?

In this Investigation, you will:

1 Accurately measure changes in temperature.

2 Develop a way to convert between Fahrenheit and Celsius temperature scales.

In the reading you learned that materials expand as the temperature increases. You will observe this phenomenon and quantify it, using both the Fahrenheit and Celsius temperature scales. You will measure the temperature of water with both types of thermometers. You will graph Celsius temperature scale as a function of Fahrenheit temperature scale. From your graph you will develop a mathematical formula to convert between Fahrenheit and Celsius temperature scales.

Safety Tip: If you are using glass thermometers, remember that they are very fragile and may break. Handle them very carefully.

1 **Which cup is warmest?**

1 In front of you are four cups of water at different temperatures, marked A, B, C, and D. By dipping your finger into the water, identify each cup from hottest to coldest.

2 Place your right index finger in the hottest cup. At the same time, place your left index finger in the coldest cup. Leave them there for 30 seconds. Now place both fingers into the room temperature cup. Describe how each finger feels. Which finger feels hot? Which finger feels cold?

2 **What is the actual temperature of each cup?**

1 Using your thermometer, find the temperature in each of the cups. Do this measurement in degrees Fahrenheit. If you do not have a Fahrenheit thermometer, use the picture on the next page to convert your Celsius measurement to Fahrenheit. Record your data in the table below.

2 Now measure the water in degrees Celsius and record your data in the table on the next page.

Cup	°C	°F
A		
B		
C		
D		

3 | ## Analyzing your data

Graph your Fahrenheit vs. Celsius data. Place your Fahrenheit data on the *y*-axis and the Celsius data on the *x*-axis. Draw a best-fit line. Find the slope of the line and the linear model for your data points. Your model should be in the form of y = mx+b.

a. Based on your graph, what is the equation that allows you to convert from Celsius to Fahrenheit?

b. From the model you just obtained (°F = m°C + b), transform the formula to convert Fahrenheit to Celsius temperature.

c. Is it possible to obtain negative values of °F? Of °C? Explain your answer.

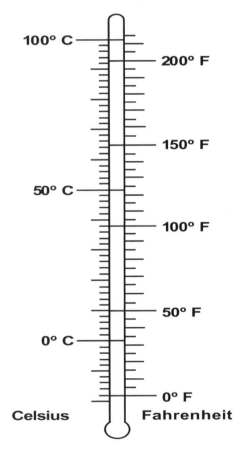

Celsius and Fahrenheit scales compared

26.2 Measuring Changes in Heat

Question: How efficient is an immersion heater?

In this Investigation, you will:

1   Calculate an increase in thermal energy, work output, work input and efficiency.
2   Analyze the efficiency of a household product.

You know that when heat is added to an object it increases its temperature. This increase depends on the mass of the object and the quantity of energy put into the object. In this Investigation, you will observe the heating of water as electrical energy is converted into thermal energy. You will use this data to calculate the efficiency of an immersion water heater.

1   **Setting up**

1   👓   Put on your goggles.
2   Attach the immersion heater to the side of your beaker.
    ⬦ **Warning: DO NOT plug the immersion heater in until it is immersed in water.**
3   Now you are going to fill the breaker with water. Using a graduated cylinder, measure how many milliliters of cold tap water it takes to cover the entire heating element. Record the volume of water in Table 1.
4   Calculate the mass of the water. Remember that each milliliter of water has a mass of 1 gram.
5   Your teacher will tell you the power of your heater in watts. Record this in Table 1.
6   Take an initial temperature reading of the water. Record this in Table 2.
7   Make sure your setup is near an electrical outlet.Reset your stopwatch.

Table 1: Initial data

Volume of water (mL)	Mass of water (g)	Heater power (watts)

👓🧤**Safety Tip: The immersion heater will get very hot. Do not touch the metal, only the handle. Also, while heating the water, you should wear goggles.**

2   Heating the water and measuring temperature

After you plug in your immersion heater, you will take temperature readings every 30 seconds. Be sure to stir the water before each measurement. Record the time and temperature in Table 2. You will not notice a significant change in temperature for the first minute. Why do you think this is?

 Unplug your immersion heater when you are finished taking data.

Table 2: Water temperature

Time (s)	Temperature (°C)
0	
30	
60	
90	
120	
150	
180	
210	
240	
270	
300	

3   Graphing your data

a. Graph the data in Table 2. On which axis will you plot temperature? On which axis will plot time?

b. Calculate the slope of your graph. Use the correct units.

c. What factors does the slope of your graph depend on?

4   # Calculating increase in thermal energy

Calculate the increase in thermal energy of the water for each minute of the experiment. Follow the directions below and record your answers in Table 3.

a. Determine the change in temperature over the course of each minute and record in Table 3.

b. Record the mass of the water from Table 1.

c. Calculate the increase in thermal energy in calories. Remember the increase in thermal energy in calories is equal to the mass times the heating constant times the change in temperature.

$$Q = mc\Delta T$$

When we are calculating the energy in calories, the heating constant is $1 \frac{\text{calorie}}{\text{gram} \, {}^{\circ}\text{C}}$. Record the increases in thermal energy for each minute in Table 3.

d. Now convert the energy into joules. Since 1 calorie = 4.186 Joules, all you need to do is multiply the energy in calories times 4.186.

Table 3: Increase in thermal energy of the water

Minute	Change in temperature (°C)	Mass of water (g)	Increase in thermal energy (calories)	Increase in thermal energy (joules)
1				
2				
3				
4				
5				

5   # Analyzing the data

a. If you were to change the mass of the water, what effect do you think this would have on the increase in thermal energy? What effect would it have on the increase in temperature?

b. What effect would changing the mass have on the slope of your graph? Draw a dashed line showing what you think this effect would be.

c. Does the increase in energy stay constant over the duration of the experiment or does it change? If it changes, why do you think this is?

6   Calculating the efficiency of the water heater

Now you are going to calculate how efficient your immersion heater is.

- **Work output** is the increase in thermal energy of the water in joules. You can get this value from Table 3. Record the values for work output for each minute in Table 4.

- **Work input** can be calculated from the definition of **power**: You are going to use the power of the immersion heater as measured in watts from Table 1. Use 60 seconds for the time value. Record your calculations in Table 4.

$$work\ input\ =\ power \times change\ in\ time$$

- To calculate the **efficiency**, simply take the work output divided by the work input. Multiply that value by 100 to express the efficiency as a percentage.

$$efficiency\ =\ \left(\frac{work\ output}{work\ input}\right) \times 100$$

Table 4: Efficiency

Minute	Work output (joules)	Power (watts) from Table 1	Work input (watts/second)	Efficiency (%)
1				
2				
3				
4				
5				

a. How efficient would you say this method of heating water is?

b. Is there any way to recapture the heat that is not absorbed by the water? What happens to the heat that the water does not absorb?

26.3 **Specific Heat**

Question: How much heat flows between liquids at different temperatures?

In this Investigation, you will:

1 Use scientific tools to make accurate measurement of temperature.

2 Investigate heat flow between liquids of different temperatures.

When you mix liquids of two different temperatures, what is the final temperature of the mixture? In this Investigation, you will determine how much heat is lost or gained when you mix two liquids of different temperatures.

1 Mixing different combinations of hot and cold water

You will conduct the following 3 experiments:

- **Experiment 1**: 250 mL hot water + 250 mL cold water
- **Experiment 2**: 500 mL hot water + 250 mL cold water
- **Experiment 3**: 250 mL hot water + 500 mL cold water

The procedures for each experiment are as follows:

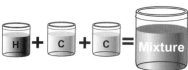

1 Do one experiment at a time. Obtain your beakers of water from your teacher before you do each experiment.

2 Use your thermometer to measure the **initial temperature** of each beaker of water. Record your results in Table 1.

3 Predict the **equilibrium temperature** and record it in Table 1. The equilibrium temperature is the final temperature of the water after mixing both of the beakers. In your notebook, show how you arrived at your prediction.

4 Pour both beakers into your large container and stir with a stirring rod. ◆ **Do not use your thermometer to stir the water. Doing this may damage or break the thermometer.**

5 Measure the actual equilibrium temperature using your thermometer. Record the results in Table 1.

6 ▣ After each experiment, dispose of the water by pouring it down a sink or into the container your teacher has provided. Do not pour your water back into the hot or cold containers of water.

Table 1: Temperature data

	Temperature of liquid A	Temperature of liquid B	Predicted equilibrium temperature	Actual equilibrium temperature
1	250 mL hot water:_____	250 mL cold water:_____		
2	500 mL hot water:_____	250 mL cold water:_____		
3	250 mL hot water:_____	500 mL cold water:_____		

2   Analyzing your data

a. On what basis did you make your predictions for the equilibrium temperature in each experiment?

b. How did your predicted equilibrium temperature compare to the actual equilibrium temperature in each experiment? What can you conclude about the equilibrium temperature based on your results?

c. In each experiment, how does the change in temperature of the cold water compare to the change in temperature of the warm water? Explain.

d. In each experiment, how does the change in **energy** of the cold water compare to the change in energy of the warm water? Explain.

3   Calculating heat gain

How much heat did the cold water gain? For the cold water to warm up, it had to gain energy from the hot water. How many calories of heat did the cold water gain in each experiment? Remember, it takes 1 calorie of heat to raise the temperature of 1 gram of water 1 °C. You can calculate the heat gained (Q), in calories, using the equation: $Q = mc\Delta T$. Table 2 explains the variables in the equation.

Table 2: Variables in the heat gain equation

variable	definition	units	How you get the variable
m	mass of water	grams	The mass of water can be calculated from the volume. Remember that 1 mL of water has a mass of 1 gram.
c	heating constant, or specific heat	$\frac{calorie}{gram°C}$	For water the specific heat is $1\frac{calorie}{gram°C}$
ΔT	change in temperature of the cold liquid	°C	$\Delta T = T_{equilibrium} - T_{cold}$

Use Table 3 to calculate heat gain, Q, for each experiment.

Table 3: Calculating heat gain

	$m_{cold\ water}$	c_{water}	$T_{equilibrium}$	$T_{cold\ water}$	ΔT	$Q_{heat\ gain}$
1		$1\frac{calorie}{gram°C}$				
2		$1\frac{calorie}{gram°C}$				
3		$1\frac{calorie}{gram°C}$				

4 ## Calculating heat loss

How much heat did the hot water lose? Calculating heat loss is like calculating heat gain. You still use the equation, $Q = mc\Delta T$, where Q is heat loss, in calories. In this case, the change in temperature is the difference between the equilibrium temperature and the temperature of the hot water: $\Delta T = T_{equilibrium} - T_{hot}$. Calculate the heat lost by the hot water. Record your answers in Table 4.

Table 4: Calculating heat loss

	$m_{hot\ water}$	c_{water}	$T_{equilibrium}$	$T_{hot\ water}$	ΔT	$Q_{heat\ loss}$
1		$1\,\dfrac{calorie}{gram\,°C}$				
2		$1\,\dfrac{calorie}{gram\,°C}$				
3		$1\,\dfrac{calorie}{gram\,°C}$				

5 ## What happened to the heat in the experiment?

a. According to the law of conservation of energy, the amount of heat/energy gained by the cold water should be equal to the amount of heat/energy lost by the hot water. Compare the heat gained by the cold water to the heat lost by the hot water. Are they equal in each experiment?

b. If the heat gain is not equal to the heat loss, what do you think happened to the missing heat?

6 ## Mixing hot water and cold alcohol

For this experiment, you will need 250 milliliters of hot water and 250 milliliters of cold alcohol.

◆ **Safety Tip: The alcohol used in this experiment is toxic if ingested.**

1 Measure the temperature of each liquid and record the temperatures in Table 5.

2 Predict the equilibrium temperature of the mixture of these two liquids and record in Table 5. Show your work in your notebook. Remember to pour both beakers into you large container.

3 Stir the mixture with your stirring rod for a few seconds.

4 Measure the actual equilibrium temperature of the new mixture. Was the equilibrium temperature weighted closer to the water or alcohol? Based on your answer, which liquid do you think has a higher specific heat?

Table 5: Mixing hot water and cold alcohol

Temperature of hot water	Temperature of cold alcohol	Predicted equilibrium temperature	Actual equilibrium temperature

7 ## Calculating heat lost by the water

Use the equation $Q = mc\Delta T$ to calculate the heat lost by the hot water.

Table 6: Heat lost by hot water in alcohol mixture

$m_{hot\ water}$	c_{water}	$T_{equilibrium}$	$T_{hot\ water}$	ΔT	$Q_{heat\ loss}$
	$1\frac{calorie}{gram°C}$				

8 ## Determining the heat gained by the alcohol

Since we do not know the specific heat of alcohol, we cannot calculate the heat gained by the alcohol using the same method we used for water. However, based on the previous three experiments, we can confidently assume that the heat lost by the hot fluid is approximately equal to the heat gained by the warm liquid. Based on the results of all of the experiments, how much heat did the alcohol gain?

9 ## Challenge!

a. Can you figure out the specific heat of the alcohol? Hint: Start with the equation $Q = mc\Delta T$. You can rearrange the variables and solve for c, specific heat. You will also need to know the mass of 250 mL of alcohol. Your teacher will have that information for you.

b. The alcohol used in this experiment is isopropyl alcohol. How does the specific heat of isopropyl alcohol compare with those of methyl alcohol (methanol) and ethyl alcohol (ethanol)? Use a chemistry manual to look up the values for all of these types of alcohol.

c. How does the specific heat for isopropyl alcohol that you derived compare to the value from the chemistry manual? How could you design this experiment to obtain better results?

27.1 Conduction

Question: How well do common materials conduct heat?

In this Investigation, you will:

1 Investigate conduction in common materials.

2 Compare heat conduction in several materials and then rank their thermal conductivity.

It turns out that the different states of matter — solid, liquid, gas — conduct heat at different rates. Which state of matter conducts heat fastest? Which state of matter conducts heat most slowly? As you answer these questions, consider the process of conduction and also consider your own experiences with conduction that may involve different states of matter. The most important thing is that you defend your answers with either a logical argument based on what you know or have just learned about conduction, or with observations about heat transfer.

1 Observing common materials

Your teacher has arranged a set of materials for you to touch. Touch each material briefly and record if it "feels" warm, cool, or in-between.

Material	Apparent temperature, according to touch	Thermal conductivity ranking

2 Determining which materials are conductors and which are insulators

a. You probably found that the materials feel like when they are at different temperatures. However, all these objects are in this room and are at the same temperature. Explain why materials *feel* like they are at different temperatures even though they are not. To answer this, you have to think about the process of conduction as heat is transferred from your hand to each material.

Question: In the table above, rank these four materials in terms of their thermal conductivity. Thermal conductivity is the ability of a material to conduct heat. You may need to compare the materials several times as you try to rank them. Use a 1 to 4 scale with a "1" being the least able to conduct heat and "4" being the most able to conduct heat.

3 　🔍 **Extension: calculating heat loss or gain through a classroom wall**

Keeping our homes and schools warm or cool as needed is very important. Consequently, we use a lot of energy for both heating and cooling. Reducing the conduction of heat through our buildings helps to lower the use of energy.

U factors indicate how well a particular material or combination of materials **conducts** the flow of heat. U factors make calculations of heat transfer through a building easy to do.

In this part of the Investigation, you will use U factors of your classroom wall to calculate how much heat is lost or gained by conduction through an external wall of a classroom. Record your data and work in your lab notebook.

1　Measure temperature in the classroom the day before the activity is to be done, in °F.

2　Look up yesterday's high and low temperatures in the newspaper and find yesterday's average temperature. A commonly accepted method for finding average temperature is simply to add the high and low temperatures together and divide by 2.

3　Measure the square area of all the wall space in the exterior wall of your classroom, excluding windows.

4　Materials used in buildings, and wall, roof and floor materials, are ranked by thermal conductivity, called *heat transfer coefficient U factors*. Your teacher will give you the U factor of your wall material. Record this value.

5　The heat transfer equation is $Q = U \times A \times \Delta t$. Q is the heat in Btu's transferred per hour, *U* is the U factor, *A* is the area in square feet. and Δt is the difference in temperature between the inside and outside in °F.

6　Use the heat transfer equation to calculate heat loss or gain through the wall material.

7　Repeat steps 3-5, this time measuring the heat loss through the windows in the exterior wall.

8　Add the heat gain or loss through windows and walls together to calculate the entire heat gain or loss through the classroom exterior wall, per hour of the previous day.

9　Multiply by 24 hours/day to get the entire day's heat gain or loss through the wall material.

4 　**What did you learn?**

a.　Compare the heat transfer through the wall with the heat transfer through the windows.

b.　With your group, brainstorm ways you could reduce heat loss or gain in your classroom.

27.2 Convection

Question: How much heat is transferred through convection?

In this Investigation, you will:

1 Investigate convection through liquids.
2 Observe convection through liquids.

You have learned that natural convection occurs by the movement of a hot gas or liquid into a region of colder gas or liquid. Forced convection occurs when a gas or liquid is forced (by either pressure or a fan) into another gas or liquid. In this Investigation, you will quantitatively observe the vertical movement of colored water due to temperature differences. You will also qualitatively observe forced convection.

1 Doing the experiment

1 Have your stopwatch ready. You will start your stopwatch at the end of the setup.
2 Arrange the glass tubing in the stopper as seen in Figure 1.
3 Your teacher will provide you with hot water. Fill the flask with the hot water and mix in food coloring. Stir completely. Be very careful since the water might be very hot!
4 Measure the temperature of the hot water and record in Table 1.
5 Very carefully insert the glass tubing-stopper arrangement into the neck of the flask. You should hold the flask with a wet paper towel.
6 Place the hot water flask into the large beaker. Again, hold the flask with a wet paper towel.
7 Fill the large beaker with room-temperature water. As you fill the beaker, measure how much water you use. Fill the beaker until the water is about ½ centimeter above the higher pipette.
8 Record the volume and temperature of the water you used in Table 1.

👓🧤 **Safety Tip: Wear your goggles and use a potholder or a wet paper towel to hold the hot-water flask!**

Table 1: Initial data

Temp. of hot water:_____ °C	Volume water in large beaker:_____ mL
	Temp. of water in large beaker:_____ °C

2 Data and observations

1 Record the time and temperature of the water in the outer beaker when convection starts.
2 Take temperature readings every minute until three minutes after convection stops. Record your data in Table 2. In the third column, mark (Yes/No) if convection is occurring. It is important to note at what time convection stops.

3   In your notebook, record your observations 1 minute after the onset of convection. You may also sketch your observations.

4   In your notebook, record your observations 5 minutes after the onset of convection. You may also sketch your observations.

Table 2: Convection data

Time	Temp.	Y/N	Time	Temp.	Y/N	Time	Temp.	Y/N

3 How much heat was transferred by convection?

Calculate the amount of heat transferred using the equation $Q = mc\Delta T$.

$m_{cold\ water}$	c_{water}	T_{final}	$T_{initial}$	ΔT	$Q_{heat\ transferred}$
	$1\,\dfrac{calorie}{gram°C}$				

a.   What is the rate of heat transfer? Divide heat transferred by time.

b.   What do you think of these results? Does natural convection seem like a good method for transferring heat?

c.   How much heat was transferred in the one minute after convection stopped? What was this rate of heat transfer?

d.   If convection has stopped, and there was no mixing, what caused this additional heat transfer?

e.   How does this other method of heat transfer compare with convection? Explain.

4 Forced convection

Now you are going to repeat the experiment in a different way.

1   Obtain another flask full of colored water and place it in the empty large beaker.

2   Fill the large beaker with water. You do not need to measure the amount of water you put in this time. Pour in just enough water so the level of the water covers the lower pipette but not the upper pipette. The water level should be at least ½ inch below the level of the upper pipette.

3   Take your straw and place it 1 cm either inside or outside the pipette, depending on how it best fits. If it looks like it is not a tight seal, use a piece of tape from your teacher.

4   Now, blow *gently* through the straw. As you do this, the other members in your group can draw a picture of the resulting forced convection.

5   Describe and record your observations. How is forced convection similar or different from natural convection?

Question: Which materials are good absorbers of radiation?

In this Investigation, you will:

1 Analyze the radiation absorption of different materials.

2 Make conclusions about the absorptive properties of a substance.

Heat can be transferred by electromagnetic radiation. In this Investigation, you will expose water and soil to radiation from a light bulb and measure the temperature of each as a function of time. You will identify which of the materials is the best absorber of radiation.

1   Setting up

Obtain the light bulb assembly from your teacher, plug it into an electrical outlet and turn it on.

◈ Safety Tip: Once plugged in, the light bulb gets very hot.

You will need to add food coloring to one of your beakers. You will be adding sand and dirt to the other beakers.

Set up and label the following beakers:

- **#1**: empty (air).

- **#2**: 200 milliliters water.

- **#3**: 200 mL water with dark food coloring.

- **#4**: 200 mL light sand.

- **#5**: 200 mL dark sand or dark soil.

2   Doing the experiment

1 Measure the initial temperature of the substance in each beaker. Record the data in Table 1 in the column labeled $T_{initial}$.

2 Place the light bulb a measured distance over the first beaker. Make sure that your light bulb is the same distance from the beaker in each experiment. Leave the bulb over the beaker for 5 minutes. Measure the temperature of the air in the beaker at the end of 5 minutes. Record this data in Table 1 in the column labelled T_{warmed}.

3 Now move the light bulb to the next beaker. Again, you will measure the temperature of the substance in that beaker after it has warmed for 5 minutes. While you are waiting, calculate the change in temperature due to absorption and record your calculation in Table 1 in the column labeled $T_{change\ 1}$

4   As the substance in the next beaker warms up, the substance in the previous beaker will cool down. Measure the temperature of the substance after it has cooled for 10 minutes and record this in Table 1 in the column marked T_{cooled}.

5   Again, calculate the temperature change ($T_{cooled} - T_{change\ 1}$) and record it in Table 1, in the column labeled $T_{change\ 2}$

3 Recording the data

Table 1: Temperature data

Beaker	$T_{initial}$	T_{warmed}	$T_{change\ 1}$	T_{cooled}	$T_{change\ 2}$
1					
2					
3					
4					
5					

4 Analyzing the data

In Table 2, rank the five substances according to how fast they heat and cool. The table is set up to list the materials from left to right, from quickest at heating and cooling to slowest at heating and cooling.

Table 2: Rating substances on ability to heat and cool

Quickest at heating and cooling 1	2	3	4	Slowest at heating and cooling 5

a.   How does the increase in temperature of the plain water compare with the increase in temperature of the colored water? Why do you think this is? What about the cooling of those two fluids?

b.   How does the increase in temperature of the light sand compare with that of the dark dirt? How does the cooling of the materials compare?

c.   What conclusions can you make about the relationship between color and the absorptive properties of a substance?

d.   How does the increase in temperature of the water compare with the increase in temperature of the sand? What other factors besides absorptive properties are responsible for these differences?

Weather

Question: How does heating and cooling affect the weather?

In this Investigation, you will:

1 Analyze weather patterns as a result of heating and cooling of the Earth's atmosphere.
2 Interpret weather maps.

You have read about how the Earth and the atmosphere above it are affected by heating and cooling. You have learned how the sun heats the Earth and how the heating of land is different than the heating of water. Based on your readings, you are going to analyze the national weather forecast and try to make deductions as to what causes differences in weather across the nation.

1 Analyzing temperature

Your teacher has provided you with a national weather forecast from a daily newspaper. Locate the list of the temperature and sky cover in cities around the country. Also, locate the weather map showing where it is sunny, the temperature, high- and low-pressure regions, and fronts. Begin the Investigation by recording the high and low temperatures for cities in the table below.

City	High	Low	Temp difference	Sky cover	Pressure
Seattle					
Los Angeles					
Las Vegas					
Phoenix					
Atlanta					
Tampa					
San Francisco					
Oklahoma City					
New Orleans					
Kansas City					
Tucson					
Denver					
Dallas					
Houston					

City	High	Low	Temp difference	Sky cover	Pressure
Minneapolis					
Memphis					
Chicago					
Miami					
New York					
Baltimore					

2 How does location affect the temperature?

Use the table in step 1 to respond to the following.

a. Give examples of differences in heating by latitude. Explain why these differences exist.

b. Give examples of differences in the high temperature by geography. Include in your explanation mention of geographical features such as the Pacific Ocean, the Rocky Mountains, the Great Lakes, and the Atlantic Ocean. Explain why geography influences temperatures.

c. Give examples of changes in the temperature difference between different types of topography (such as dry desert, forest, coastal region, swamp land). Explain why topography influences temperature differences.

d. Fill in the table for the sky cover for each city. How does the sky cover affect the temperature? Why do you think this is?

e. On your weather map, what states do the areas of high pressure center on? Which states do the low-pressure areas center on?

f. In the fifth column, record whether you think each city is in a region of high pressure, low pressure, or in-between.

g. What kind of cloud cover or weather is associated with high-pressure regions? Look at the sky cover for the cities in the high-pressure regions. What do you think the humidity is like in these regions?

h. What kind of cloud cover or weather is associated with low-pressure regions? Look at the sky cover for the cities in the high-pressure regions. What do you think the humidity is like in these regions?

i. The barbs on the fronts on the weather map tell us the direction of the wind. The cold fronts are symbolized by triangles, the warm fronts by semicircles. Are fronts associated with high- or low-pressure regions? What is the weather like in a front?

j. Based on what you have read about low- and high-pressure regions, let's investigate what effect they have on the wind. High-pressure regions tend to push wind toward low-pressure regions. Do you think the air in a low-pressure region tends to sink or rise? Does the air in a high-pressure region sink or rise?

k. Based on those conclusions, how do you think low-pressure regions contribute to the formation of rainstorms?

Living Systems

Question: Which types of food contain the greatest amount of energy?

In this Investigation, you will:

1 Analyze the energy content of common food items.

2 Compare the energy content of common food items.

Different types of food provide different amounts of energy to sustain our daily activities. This energy comes from a process called cellular respiration which occurs in our cells. In this Investigation, you will estimate the amount of energy some foods release. Which of these foods will give you the most energy? Which of these foods have the most calories? You will estimate the energy of three different pieces of food.

1   Doing the experiment

◈ **Safety Tip: Be very careful using the matches and handling the cans with hot water. Do this activity in a well ventilated area, since the fumes from burning the food are strong.**

Your teacher has given you three pieces of food. Based on what you know about these foods, write a hypothesis in your notebook about which of the foods contains the most energy per gram.

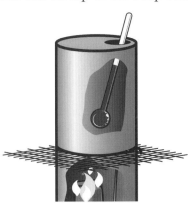

Marshmallow

Paper clip

1 Bend a large paper clip, as shown in the figure to the right, so that it can hold the food items in a steel soup can.

2 Use a balance to measure the mass of the piece of food. Record it in your data table.

3 Suspend the piece of food in the paper clip support.

4 Use a graduated cylinder to measure 100 ml of tap water. Pour it into an empty soda can.

5 Insert the thermometer through the opening of the soda can and record the initial temperature of the water in the table on the next page.

6 With a match, ignite the food. Quickly place the wire grid and the soda can on top of the soup can.

7 The food should burn completely. (If the flame goes out before it is mostly burned, empty the water and start all over again.) Record the temperature of the water after the food has burned completely. Allow the temperature of the water to reach its highest temperature. As the food burns, write a brief description comparing the burning of the different foods (*i.e.*, was the burning slow, fast, large flames, smoky?).

8 Empty the water and repeat the process with the other food items.

2   **Recording your data**

Record your data from the experiment in the table below.

Food sample	Mass of sample	Initial water temp	Final water temp
	(g)	(°C)	(°C)

a. Describe the burning of the first food.

b. Describe the burning of the second food.

c. Describe the burning of the third food.

3   **Analyzing your data**

a. Using the equation $Q = mc\Delta T$, find the energy content of your food items in calories.

Item 1:

Item 2:

Item 3:

b. Convert the above answers to Calories. Remember, 1 Calorie equals 1000 calories.

Item 1:

Item 2:

Item 3:

c. Convert the above answers to joules. Remember, 1 Calorie equals 4187 joules.

Item 1:

Item 2:

Item 3:

d. Is your hypothesis supported by your data? Why or why not?

e. Your teacher will now present you with the nutritional information from the packages these items of food came in. How does the package's estimate of the Calories in the food compare with your estimate? Why do you think there is a difference?

f. How do you think you could improve your experiment to attain more accurate calorimetric data?

g. Compare the nutritional information on the ratio of proteins to carbohydrates to fat in each food item. Can you make any generalizations about the burning characteristics and calorie content of fat vs. carbohydrates?

28.3 Mechanical Systems

Question: How much energy is lost as heat in a mechanical system?_.l

In this Investigation, you will:

1 Analyze the efficiency of a mechanical system.
2 Calculate the energy lost as heat in a mechanical system.

The efficiency of mechanical systems is always less than 100 percent. That is, the work output is always less than the work input. Most of the energy lost in a machine in the form of heat due to friction. In this Investigation, you will observe the heat generated by friction and deformation.

1 Examining a rubber band

Your teacher will give you a rubber band. It is important that you use the rubber band appropriately! First, feel the rubber band to get a sense of its temperature. Then, take the rubber band and fully stretch and relax it quickly 10 times. Feel the rubber band again. What has changed? Why? What is the source of energy that caused this change?

◆**Safety Tip: Using rubber bands inappropriately is unsafe in the classroom and lab. Flying or popped rubber bands can cause seriously injury.**

2 Shaking sand in a can

1 Fill a soft drink can halfway with fine sand. Measure the temperature of the sand with your thermometer. Record the initial temperature of the sand in Table 1.

2 Cover the hole of the can with your hand and shake the can vigorously for three minutes. Measure the temperature of the sand again and record it in Table 1.

3 Why did the temperature of the sand change? What is the source of energy that caused the temperature change?

Table 1: Sand temperature data

Initial temperature of sand (°C)	Final temperature of sand (°C)

3   Extension activity: What is the best way to generate electricity?

Do you know where your electricity comes from? Do you know what kind of power plant produces it? In this long-term project, you will investigate the different methods of generating electricity. Each group in the class will research one type of power plant. When all the groups have completed their work, the class will review and discuss (or debate) the information. Each group will be responsible for providing evidence for why their particular source of energy is the best at generating electricity.

The final goal of this project is for your class to try to determine the most efficient, cost-effective, and environmentally safe method for generating electricity.

Sources of energy for generating electricity: coal, oil, natural gas, nuclear, hydroelectric, solar, wind, and geothermal.

Research:

1   Choose one of the methods for generating electricity for research.

2   Make a list of facts about this source of energy. Try to come up with at least 10 pros and 10 cons. In making your list, cover these topics:
   * How much does your energy source cost to use?
   * What is the energy efficiency of your energy source?
   * How much does it cost to build a power plant for generating energy with your source?
   * How much does it cost to maintain a power plant for generating energy with your source?
   * How does the use of your energy source affect human health?
   * What are the environmental costs or problems associated with using your energy source?
   * How long will this source last into the future?

3   As you make your list of pros and cons, fill in details that explain each point.

4   When you have researched your energy source, compile a list of facts about the other energy sources that explain why they are less favorable than your source.

5   Organize your information so that your group will be well prepared for the class discussion. Study this information.

$CH_4 + 2O_2 \rightarrow 2H_2O + CO_2 +$ energy
Chemical energy

Heat energy

Hot steam

Mechanical energy

Electrical energy

Class discussion/debate:

After you have completed your research, you and your group will participate in a class discussion or debate. Your teacher will provide you with the details of this part of the Investigation.

Where to find information:

- www.energy.gov
- www.ase.org
- www.energy.ca.gov

- www.fe.doe.gov/education/index.html
- www.eia.doe.gov
- www.ne.doe.gov

- www.ott.doe.gov/biofuels
- www.inel.gov/national/hydropower/index.html
- www.eren.doe.gov